Enjoy Life

by
exercising
a fit & healthy mind

STEVE MILLS
www.fitandhealthymind.com

First Published in 2012 by:

Fit and Healthy Mind Limited

ISBN: 978-0-9574226-0-5

www.fitandhealthymind.com

enjoylife@fitandhealthymind.com

Designed by Vicky Mills

http://www.behance.net/vickymills

To all who want to Enjoy Life

CONTENTS

1. INSPIRATION

Have you ever had feelings that although life is pretty okay, it could be better? Have there been times when it hasn't been okay and you haven't known how to rediscover life enjoyment? Do you wish there was a practical way to really enjoy life to the full, every day? These have been the questions that have kept resurfacing in my mind during recent years.

But in my fiftieth year, I have discovered a new way of thinking that has transformed my life enjoyment. This book has been written not as an attempt to persuade you to adopt this way of thinking and living, but is shared in the spirit of 'it has worked for me, it may help you too'.

Had everything, but not enjoyment…

The change was prompted by a recognition that I had everything I needed to enjoy life to the full, but wasn't. I had good health, a well paid and interesting career which took me across the world lecturing on marketing, a strong and loving family, a big house, new cars, overseas holidays and no debts. Everything you would expect should have meant I had reached utopia. Life should have been as enjoyable as it can get. Yet it wasn't. I couldn't honestly say at the end of each day that I had enjoyed that day to the full. I was still worrying about things. I still got frustrated and annoyed when things didn't go to plan. I still became angry. I still found myself wanting more. I was still striving for that next exotic holiday, better car or work contract that would put the final icing on the cake.

Reflection on what was missing

So I spent a lot of time reflecting on what was missing. What could transform my life from reasonably okay to really enjoyable? I read lots of material about self-development, finding real happiness, having a more positive outlook and developing a more spiritual perspective. I chatted at length with family and friends. I attended meditation sessions at a Buddhist centre. They all seemed to offer partial solutions, but none provided the holistic life enjoyment approach I was seeking.

New approach

So drawing inspiration from all these sources, I have put together my own philosophy on how to enjoy life, based on exercising a fit and healthy mind. It provides a new lens on life. And now I'd like to share it because it might be as life transforming for you as it has been for me.

The book starts by exploring what 'enjoy life' really means and the importance of experiencing it now. It then looks at the components of a fit and healthy body and how they provide a perfect parallel for developing a fit and healthy mind. A series of practical and energising exercises for the mind are then offered, to help enjoy life to the full.

It's worth being clear from the outset that my qualifications for writing this book are not academic. No PhDs in psychiatry, psychology or neuroscience. Rather, the approach is grounded in reflections about real life, my own and those around me, giving a perspective which is fresh, pragmatic and practical.

To make it a more engaging read, the book has been written in the style of a dialogue between myself and a good friend, Paul.

Enjoy!

2. DISCOVERING A MORE ENJOYABLE LIFE

Paul: Steve, you seem to have changed. It's still you, but a better version of you. A you that seems much more at one with himself and with everyone else.

Steve: I know this sounds a bit sensationalist, but I do feel transformed. A new life, or maybe the life that I could have been leading for the past 50 years, now just discovered.

Paul: So what's behind the change?

Steve: It's actually very simple. I've just adopted an approach of 'Enjoy Life by Exercising a Fit and Healthy Mind'. That's it. And it has meant that I now have a mind that is filled with more positive thoughts. Many things that previously used to worry, frustrate or irritate me, no longer do. I'm more content, more fulfilled, more relaxed and generally more happy.

Paul: Tell me more...

Enjoy life

Steve: Let's start with 'Enjoy Life'.

I realised that whatever else you think you want from life, in terms of career success, material things, exotic holidays, friends or family, the single most important thing that we all really want is an Enjoyable Life. To be able to say at the point of death: 'I really enjoyed my life to the full'.

Yet, very few people are able to say those few words with honesty. This is clearly articulated in a book called 'The Top Five Regrets of the Dying' by Bronnie Ware. That final point of reflection is filled with regrets about what life should have been like, what they should have done, what they wasted too much time and effort doing and what they didn't realise was really important until it was too late. Religious beliefs aside, you only get one chance. There are 7 billion lives happening at any one time, but you only get one of them; and it's disappearing by the minute.

Fit and healthy mind

P: Strong stuff, but where does the 'Fit and Healthy Mind' part come in?

S: It is only by exercising a Fit and Healthy Mind that we can experience real enjoyment. In a nutshell, this means a mind that is oxygenated with positive thoughts rather than toxic negative ones. It's a mind that has developed strong and resilient mental muscles that can resist negative emotions like stress, anger and jealousy. It's a flexible mind that can easily respond to different challenges in a fluid and adaptable, but balanced way. And finally, it's a mind that is lean and lucid rather than flabby and overburdened with the baggage of previous unhealthy thoughts.

P: So you seem to be drawing an analogy between the benefits of a fit and healthy body and a fit and healthy mind.

S: Exactly. And the parallels are both instructive and inspirational. We just need to think about all the guidance which exists for developing a fit and healthy body and draw on it to help develop a fit and healthy mind.

An OK life

P: So how is this any different from my life? I reckon I pretty much enjoy it. Okay, it has its ups and downs, but hey, that's life! I have a laugh. I may have the odd disappointment too, but who doesn't? Most of the time things go to plan. And where they don't, we get over it. No real problems. There are the annoying neighbours I suppose, but we just try to block them out and ignore them. Hopefully they'll move soon. No real hang-ups. Bit concerned about how my son is doing in his school exams, but the children can't all be geniuses like their dad! Things are going reasonably well in my career. Not the top man, but to be frank I don't want to be. Who needs even more stress? Keep my head down and hopefully they won't notice me until I can enjoy a well-earned retirement. We have some pretty good family holidays. Okay the odd one that hasn't gone totally to plan, but you can't always control the weather and the strikes at Paris airport. My football team is winning, well some of the time at least!

S: So life's OK?

P: Yes, definitely.

S: Fully enjoyable or just OK?

P: Good enough.

S: And you're happy with that? 'A good enough, OK life'?

P: It's as good as anyone else I know, and certainly better than those poor people in Africa or even in this country who haven't got a job. So be happy with your lot I say, and just get on with it.

Change your mind's response

S: Fine. But you could have so much more enjoyment in your life. Real enjoyment. Not through having to change any of the external situations, but by changing the way your mind interprets and responds to them.
    The great thing about 'Enjoying Life by exercising a Fit and Healthy Mind' is that it costs nothing. It doesn't require anyone else to do anything different. It doesn't mean any changes to what your son does, or the neighbours do, or your football team does, or even what the French do! Nothing external needs to change at all. The only change is internal.

P: Not sure I totally get you.

S: A fundamental principle is that enjoyment doesn't come from the external. It comes from our mind's response to the external.

P: So you're suggesting that I don't get enjoyment from watching my team play?

S: Well do you?

P: I do when they win!

S: And when they lose?

P: I feel down and despondent for the rest of the weekend. Unfortunately, the way they played last season, I was more down than up. But that's what being a true fan is about.

S: But just step back from this for a second. Your emotions, high and low, are being controlled by eleven men kicking a round leather object for 90 minutes. Is that how you want life to be? At that deathbed moment, do you really want to think about all those Saturday evenings you wasted because you felt down about a group of footballers not playing very well? Or because a man dressed in black with a whistle had a different view from you?

P: But that's what being a football supporter is about. That's what you do. You enjoy the highs and you get over the lows. If you can't handle it, don't support a football team!

S: I also support a football team, and they lose a lot more often than your's! But the point I'm making is that we are allowing our emotions to be controlled by an external event. If we were to exercise a more fit and healthy mind we could control those emotions. We don't need to feel disappointed and down when they lose. Not every supporter of our team will have exactly the same emotional response. Some will be more upset and annoyed, whilst others will shrug it off.

P: So your point is?

External events don't need to dictate our emotions

S: My point is that the external event does not need to dictate the emotional response. If it did, we would all have exactly the same emotional reaction to whatever happens. But we don't. Our emotional responses are different. And the key point is that with a fit and healthy mind, we can choose the emotional response we want to have to any external stimulus or situation.

P: So you're suggesting I remain neutral, win or lose?

S: No, not at all. This is not about neutralising emotions. Celebrate and enjoy their wins. But with a fit and healthy mind that realises there may also be times in the future when they will lose. And when they lose, use a fit and healthy mind to still enjoy the experience.

P: Enjoy my team losing? I'm wondering if you're losing it?!

S: I know this is pushing it for an early discussion, but I assure you that if you develop a fit and healthy mind this is possible. And will lead to a greater enjoyment of life.

P: Go on.

Seeing the positives

S: A fit and healthy mind is able to put something as ultimately trivial as a football match into context. A fit and healthy mind is able to see the positives, even of a loss. It may be the team learnt some key points for a future game; it may be some junior players gained some critical experience; it may be that a formation change towards the end of the match showed a way forward for the future or that a last minute substitution would be worth bringing on earlier next time.

A fit and healthy mind is also able to appreciate the opportunity to have the time, money and freedom to watch Premier league football matches, which few people are able to do. And finally, it provides a good opportunity to develop the mind's ability to manage defeat and potential disappointment. This can stand you in better stead for when life throws some more serious personal defeats and losses your way, like failing an exam or losing out to a colleague on a job promotion.

P: OK, you may have some points. But I'm not sure I can instantly stop feeling for my team when things don't go well.

S: I'm not saying it's easy. In the same way that developing a fit and healthy body isn't easy. But through a bit of practice and effort it is possible, and the outcome of a continual sense of enjoyment of life is most definitely worth it.

P: Let me mull that over a bit more. You'll be telling me next that I shouldn't get upset by the annoying neighbours…

S: You raised it! Tell me why they annoy you.

P: Always having builders round to work on their property. I'm sure it's just to make us feel inferior. Constant noise of drilling and banging. Never an apology. Maybe if they had this fit and healthy mind you talk about, they wouldn't do it and we'd all be OK.

S: So is what they're doing annoying?

P: Obviously.

Unhealthy mind

S: Interesting, because I heard that the neighbours on the other side don't get annoyed about it at all. So that means what the 'annoying neighbours' are doing is not intrinsically annoying. You are choosing to allow your mind to interpret what they're doing as annoying. That, if you don't mind me being blunt, is down to the unhealthiness of your mind, rather than their neutral act. You have chosen the negative emotion of being annoyed. Actually, you haven't. But because you don't have control over your emotions, they have led you to the negative feeling of annoyance.

P: A bit direct, but what do you mean 'I don't have control over my emotions'? I am who I am. My emotions are part of my makeup. It's part of what makes me who I am.

S: This is a key fallacy that many people have. 'My emotions are me'. Not true...unless you want that to be the case. Unless you want to play the victim card...and if that's the case, you can abandon any hope of living a fully enjoyable life. A key point about developing a fit and healthy mind is that you can control your emotions, rather than being hostage to them.

P: Not sure I get you.

S: You don't have to feel anger, stress, jealousy, annoyance, fear, frustration or any other negative

11

emotion. You can, if you want, choose to neutralise these negative emotions and even replace them with positive enlivening ones.

P: But if the neighbours are making lots of noise…

S: You can choose whether you want that external stimulus to provoke in your mind feelings of anger, or stress, or jealousy or annoyance. Completely within your control. But be clear, what the neighbours are doing is not of itself annoying. It is simply an action by an external person or group. It's your choice about how to respond which has led you to feel a sense of annoyance.

P: But anyone would be annoyed with all that noise all the time.

Same stimulus, different responses

S: But they're not. The other neighbours say that they're not at all annoyed. In fact they have responded to exactly the same external stimulus in a completely different way. They're pleased that it will make the street more desirable to prospective purchasers and that the neighbours will be able to host the next New Year's party. Same stimulus, different responses. There is choice.

And when the other neighbours at the back had their extension, you didn't get annoyed.

P: Yeah, but I get on with them.

S: But notice what's happening. Same external stimulus, different responses. Even in your own mind. So there is choice. That means you can decide how you want to respond. Annoyance or a positive perspective.

Provided you have a fit and healthy mind to exercise that choice.

P: So how about if the neighbours had a fit and healthy mind? Then they might have had the decency to apologise in advance for the noise.

S: The key thing about a fit and healthy mind is that the start point is ourselves. We are the ones who must first develop it. Only when our mind is totally fit and healthy can we tell others to do the same.

P: I'm not sure anyone could ever have a totally fit and healthy mind.

S: That's the point!

Benefits of a fit and healthy mind

So let's focus all our efforts and energies on our own mind. That will have a number of benefits. Firstly, it will lead to a more enjoyable life. Secondly, it will enable us to respond in a mentally stronger and more positive way to others whose minds are not fit and healthy. And thirdly, some of our approach is likely to rub off on others who are attracted by our changed life orientation and more positive mind state.

P: So let me just check I get what you're saying. I have a choice about how I respond to a situation. I can choose whether to respond in a negative, neutral or positive way. I can control my emotions, rather than them controlling me. And this is the route to a more enjoyable life.

S: Yes, that's pretty much it.

P: Let's try this out with another scenario. How about last year's holiday. Not the best we've had. We were really looking forward to it. After all the hard work I'd put in during the year, we didn't deserve to have a fortnight of rain, delayed flights and one of the kids being ill. How does that fit into your enjoyment utopia?!!

S: Can I just ask, did everyone on that same holiday have as bad a time as you?

P: I guess not. Some were more upset by it all than we were, but there were a couple of families who seemed to keep on smiling. I'm not sure how they did it.

S: So there's your clue again. Same stimulus, different responses. Therefore it's not the stimulus that's the cause of your upset. It's your response to the stimulus. And that's something that could be within your control.

P: What do you mean 'could be'?

S: Well it doesn't seem that it is at the moment. You seem more controlled by the external and by your instinctive reactions and emotions. But it could be within your control if you exercised a more fit and healthy mind.

P: So you're daring to say I should have enjoyed that disastrous holiday?! What was there to enjoy?

S: Let me ask you. What was there to enjoy? Was there anything?

P: Probably not. To be honest, it's not something I've given any thought about. At the end of the day we put it down as a bad holiday and that's it.

Extract the positives

S: So just out of interest, let's see if we can extract any positives, however small. Did you all come back in good health and without any injuries? Were you all feeling in good physical health most of the time? Were you able to spend time in each other's company? Did you play any games together that brought you closer as a family? Did you have any interesting food and drink? Did you have a better time than most of the world's population who have never travelled outside of their native country, and probably never will? Did you have the opportunity to learn another language and learn about a different culture? Did you have time to read and enrich your mind?

P: Yes, yes, yes...In fact yes to them all. But that's not the point. It wasn't what we'd hoped and expected it to be.

S: Let's do this one bit at a time. There were lots of positives had you taken the time to look for them and fill your mind with them. As indeed some people were able to do and enjoyed the holiday more as a result. Same holiday, different responses, different levels of enjoyment.

Secondly, you say, it fell below your hopes and expectations.

P: Clearly.

S: Whose fault is that? Who set the hopes and expectations? The weather forecaster? The holiday brochure?

P: Yes.

Inflated mental images

S: No. They provided some external information and stimulus. But you built the hopes and expectations. They were built in your mind. This was your mental image of how the holiday should be. You chose to develop an inflated mental image and then compare it with the reality.

P: And so?

S: Which is easier to change? The reality or your mental image? It's a no-brainer. Reality is what reality is. We can try to shape certain elements of our external environment, but in the majority of cases it's actually easier to change the perspective in our mind. This is the critical point of our whole discussion. If you want to fully enjoy life, don't try to control life. You can't. Rather, work to control both your expectations of the external and your internal responses to the life that actually materialises. This is the route to a fully enjoyable life.

P: OK. This is a bit different isn't it? I'm not sure I totally get what you're saying, but there's some interesting stuff. I'm willing to spare another hour of my valuable life discussing this a bit further. Whether I'll consider it an enjoyable hour, let's wait and see…!

3. DIGGING DEEPER INTO ENJOYING LIFE

P: I've been thinking a bit more about this idea of an 'enjoyable life'. Isn't that what we're all after?

S: I guess so, but I wonder if we know what it is and how to achieve it. If you ask many people what they're looking for from life, they'll say a good job, plenty of money, a really nice house, decent car, great holidays, successful kids. Very few will actually say: 'I want an enjoyable life'.

P: Yes, but that's what they mean when they say good job, plenty of money, nice house etc. They mean an enjoyable life through these things.

S: I agree. But whilst in many people's minds the two go together, in reality they don't. Have you ever sat and watched people who are driving expensive cars, or wearing expensive clothes or are in high-powered jobs when they don't know they're being watched?

P: Can't say I make a habit of it...

Do they have it all?

S: Well it's worth doing. Because in those guard-down moments, you can see whether they're really having an enjoyable life. Do they look happy? Are they smiling? Do they look content and fulfilled? Do they seem at ease with the world and with themselves? Do they look as if they have everything they and everyone else ever wanted?

P: Probably not.

S: And when you next see a beautiful property, your dream home, just take a minute to think about what the people in that dream house are actually doing. Are they all sitting around the large oak kitchen table enjoying each moment of each other's company? Are they gathered around the family Labrador as she painlessly gives birth to another litter of perfect puppies? Are they all helping to clean the house whilst singing 'We'd love to teach the world to sing in perfect harmony'?!
   Of course they're not. Chances are they're not having one iota more enjoyment than you.

P: Interesting perspective.

S: I know I'm being deliberately extreme with this, but so often our dreams are equally extreme. We fantasise as to what our lives would be like if only we were living in that luxurious property rather than the 3-bedroom house we currently have (which, incidentally, was also a dream property for us at one time).
   And just reflect for a few minutes on the so-called celebs. Wouldn't it be great to have their lifestyle? Don't they enjoy life to the full?

Celebs have it all?

P: They certainly seem to have it all.

S: Yes, that's certainly the image they and their managers and the press may want to give. But if you had it all, would you need the drugs? If you really had it all, would you need the affairs? If you had it all, would you need to go to rehab? If you had it all, would you need the constant press attention and fan adulation? If you had it all, would you need to commit suicide? Without wishing to sound too morbid about this, how many suicides happen in luxurious houses or marble decorated hotel bathrooms?!

P: Interesting, because I'd viewed many of these as signs they were enjoying their lives to the full. Not the suicide of course, but even the rehab has a certain 'celeb coolness' about it. But you're suggesting the opposite. That these are actually signs they're not really enjoying their lives, even with all that talent. How sadly ironic.

S: Let's leave the stars and come firmly back down to earth. What about your own personal experience? Do you enjoy life any more now than when your salary was a half of what it currently is?

More salary, more enjoyment?

P: Interesting question. I've certainly got a lot more home comforts, we don't need to worry so much about paying the bills and we can go on some more holidays abroad. I like the sense of status from my new car, not to mention the pure sound quality from my state-of-the-art music system. And I reckon I get a bit more respect from other people than when I wasn't quite so well off.

S: But back to the question. Do you enjoy life any more?

P: I guess it depends on what you mean by enjoy life.

S: It's certainly more than just passing pleasures or happiness highs. It's more than the ego massaging conferred by so-called status products.

P: So how do you see it?

S: Enjoyment is always seeing and experiencing the positives of any and every situation. It's minimising those negative emotions we all have, like fear, anger, anxiety, stress, disappointment and jealousy. It's experiencing a constant sense of being at one with yourself and others. It's about appreciating the power of giving which leads to even greater levels of enjoyment for yourself and others.

P: So are you suggesting we should give up all the good things of life and live the life of a monk?

Intent is key

S: Not at all. It's all about intent and orientation. If your intent is to have as many material possessions as possible, as a route to enjoying life, you will never achieve it. But if your intent is to enjoy life through exercising a fit and healthy mind, you can have the material possessions, but won't be at all dependent on them for your enjoyment.

P: I'm not sure I get the difference.

S: As we said in our previous discussion, someone who seeks to enjoy life by exercising a fit and healthy mind finds enjoyment comes from within, not from without. It is the result of internal responses in the mind, not to whatever is happening externally. So whether they're driving a Ferrari or Ford Fiesta, they're able to enjoy life. Whether they're sunning themselves on a luxury cruise liner or sitting in a wet rowing boat, they're able to enjoy life. Whether they're dining at a Michelin-starred restaurant or eating a dry sandwich on a windy beach, they're able to enjoy life.

Not dependent on the external for enjoyment

P: So you're saying they're not dependent on the external for their internal enjoyment.

S: Exactly. And that's the critical difference. As the leadership expert, John Maxwell, says: 'Life is 10% of what happens to me and 90% of how I react to it'. This is a really powerful thought. The irony is that we tend to focus 90% of our energies on the external and only 10% on developing our mind. We've got it the wrong way around. The 90/10 principle is one worth remembering.

P: That's an interesting thought. Actually, when I come to think about it, some of the most enjoyable moments we've had have been meeting up with a few close friends and having a simple BBQ on the beach. Cost us less than £5 each. And that was actually more enjoyable than when we all went to an upmarket restaurant to celebrate one of our friend's birthdays, costing more than £50 per head.

S: Of course there's nothing wrong with eating an expensive meal. The point is about our primary intent and orientation. If it's to find enjoyment from the external, we'll sometimes succeed, but oftentimes fail. If it's to find enjoyment from within, from a fit and healthy mind, we'll most times succeed, whatever around us may fail.

P: Why do you say most times?

S: Because we'll never achieve a 100% fit and healthy mind. But the nearer we get, the more enjoyable every aspect of life will be.

P: Okay, I'm beginning to see what you're saying. And there's a certain appeal to it. But are you suggesting we should all find our enjoyment from the same things?

Enjoyment is different for different people

S: Not at all. We're all different. Some find enjoyment from the stimulus of the challenge of their work. Others find it from the stimulus of pottering in the garden. For others it's the stimulus from sport or the opportunity to climb a mountain or sail across the ocean. Or it may be a combination of these things. This is not about mandating where enjoyment should come from or what it should consist of. It's first having an intent to enjoy life by exercising a fit and healthy mind. Then, with that intent and orientation, undertaking life's activities and deriving full enjoyment from them. Not based on what they alone are providing, but based on our response to that external stimulus.

P: It's starting to make some sense. But if it's so simple, why do most people not get it? Why the constant drive to improve one's material lot?

Inbuilt compulsion to want more material goods

S: Good question. Because that's what I've also spent most of my life pursuing. And I still find it an ongoing seduction. I guess that's down to a number of factors.

For many of us, it's a natural human instinct to want more and to want to possess what we don't currently have. We see an attractive car. We can't just admire it for being an attractive car. We have an inbuilt compulsion to have it as our own. We see a beautiful beach villa. We can't just admire it for being an attractive property. We have this inherent need to make it our's. To own it. To add it to our list of flauntable assets.

We're also heavily influenced by society around us. We're fundamentally fragile human beings who seek constant endorsement and reinforcement of who we are and who we'd like to be. By buying into the consumerist society, this allows us to clothe our fragile self-images with the latest stuff and receive endorsement and reassurance from our friends and colleagues. We can boost our fragile sense of self with layers of designer clothes, accoutrements of fashion watches and mobile phones, image boosting powerful cars, computers and sound systems and the bragging experiences of exotic holidays and all-expenses-paid business trips.

Ironically, the drive to more material possessions and trappings is not the outward expression of a confident self. Rather, if we're honest with ourselves, it's the outward camouflaging and boosting of a fragile sense of self.

P: So why do you think we carry on down this road?

Material seeking cycle

S: Many of us never really consider an alternative. It's how we're brought up to believe life is. Plus, it has a certain stimulant appeal. We see something, we want that something, we get that something, it gives us a momentary high. But it then just becomes another item in the wardrobe or cupboard or photo album. So we crave new excitement, new stimulation, new highs. We see something else, we want that something, we get that something, it gives us a new momentary high. And so the cycle goes on. But each time we believe the next purchase could be the one that provides a permanently increased sense of happiness. This will be the permanent ultimate dream fulfilment. But of course that never happens. It's another vapid dream which rapidly evaporates.

Actually there's a great book on this topic by John Naish, called 'Enough'. He makes the point that we now have more of everything than we can ever use, enjoy or afford. But we are still not happy.

P: So you think many of us are unknowingly trapped in this material seeking cycle?

S: Unfortunately yes. And what further perpetuates it is that many of us tend to assess people by what we see on the outside. Someone has a bigger house, faster car, smarter clothes. Assumption - they must be well off. Related assumption - they must be enjoying life. Further related assumption - they must be enjoying life more than me. Implication - I must also try to get those things so I can also enjoy life as much as they appear to be doing.

P: And I suppose this becomes self-fuelling within society, so everyone is playing the same crazy game.

S: Precisely. Interestingly, my wife said to me yesterday that someone we know has just landed a great job. That was shorthand for it's a high income job. But will it actually be a great job? Will it be a job which provides him with a higher level of enjoyment than other people we know? Will it provide him with a greater ability to see and experience the positives of any and every situation? Will he have less negative emotions like fear, anger, anxiety, stress and jealousy? Will he experience a constant sense of being at one with himself and others? Will he have a better appreciation of the power of giving which leads to even greater levels of enjoyment for self and others? Will he at the point of death reflect and say that getting that job was the critical step in having a fully enjoyable life? I wonder.

Role of consumer goods companies

P: A lot of what you're saying relates to the chasing of material goods. So is this whole phenomenon being fuelled by the consumer goods industry?

S: To a certain extent yes. But they're not doing it maliciously. They're simply responding to the belief of many people that they can have their emotional needs satisfied by material products. It's their job to develop and promote products that can supposedly transform people's happiness. To sell the dream of more beautiful hair, whiter teeth, whiter skin, darker skin, a cooler image, a more sophisticated image or whatever human need is out there. Many people have a fragile sense of self. They are looking for ways of boosting it. Consumer goods companies skilfully tap into those emotional needs and offer a solution. Consumers are happy. They buy products that give them what they need. But it stops people really thinking about whether their core emotional needs are really being met and whether they are just pawns in the consumerist game.

P: So it is down to the activities of the consumer goods companies.

S: No, it's down to human nature. Consumer goods companies are just tapping into uncontrolled human emotions. As long as we continue to believe the route to enjoyment is more stuff, they will keep developing and marketing it.

Relationship between incomes and life enjoyment

P: But on a slightly different tangent, is there not a relationship between incomes and life enjoyment?

S: Yes there is research which shows that at the lowest income levels that is the case. There are many millions who struggle to earn enough money to survive, to feed and clothe their families, to provide basic shelter, to have basic hygiene and sanitation and to access clean water. Their ability to enjoy life is severely hampered. That's not to say it's impossible, since many of these people have, despite their circumstances, developed a positive view on life and make the most of their difficult external situation.

P: Does this not contradict what you've been saying?

S: No. Because above a basic income threshold this direct correlation no longer exists. A person's income rises, but their enjoyment remains the same. Or it often drops, as the extra work and stress involved in earning yet higher incomes leads to a reduction in life enjoyment. But the problem is that in our minds we believe this direct correlation between incomes and enjoyment applies at all levels.

P: So if people saw through the mirage of enjoyment through material goods, they might be attracted to enjoying life by exercising a fit and healthy mind?

Not a quick fix solution

S: Maybe. But there's a further barrier. It's not a quick fix, buy-it-off-the-shelf, readymade solution. Developing a fit and healthy mind takes effort and self-discipline. Although less effort than the never ending treadmill of consumerism. Maybe it doesn't give those instant stimulant highs of hearing people say: 'What a beautiful house' or 'I'd love to have a car like that' or 'what model iPhone have you got?' or 'you must be really smart to do that job'.

P: So pulling all this together, what you're saying is that our minds are hardwired to believe that more stuff equals more enjoyment. And yet, if we step back and reflect on our own lives and those who seem to have it all, this is not actually the case. But because of our fragile sense of self and the fact that everyone else is doing it, we're mentally trapped in this revolving material cycle.

S: That's pretty much it.

P: So how do you break free? How do you develop this fit and healthy mind you keep talking about?

S: Let's come to that shortly. Before that, can we take a quick diversion to talk about death?

P: Seems strange, but if that's what you feel you need to do…

4. A QUICK DIVERSION TO DISCUSS DEATH

P: So why when we're talking about how to enjoy life do you want to discuss something as morbid as death?

S: Because as strange as it may sound, you can only really appreciate life once you've fully accepted death.

P: Go on.

Life is a once in a lifetime opportunity

S: Death helps frame life. Only once you accept you're going to die, do you realise the importance of life. That it's a once in a lifetime opportunity. Literally.

There is no other life. Yes there are 7 billion of them, but as far as you and I are concerned there is only one. And that one is vulnerable, fragile and decaying.

We have each, against the odds, the tremendous opportunity to spend a possible 80 years on this earth.

And then that's it. Life will go on, but our's won't. What happens after our death is academic. We may have our name engraved on a big statue or on a little seat with a view. Or on a simple stick or stone. But it is actually of no consequence to us whatsoever.

P: Actually you remind me of that Steve Jobs' quote: 'there's no point being the richest man in the graveyard'.

S: Or the most artistic, or the most intelligent, or the most musically accomplished, or the fastest, or the most politically astute, or the best dressed. When death comes, anything that happened in life is meaningless. We are all corpses decaying at the same rate, never again to experience anything.

P: But surely people with religious views wouldn't subscribe to this.

S: Whatever beliefs people may have about an afterlife, they can agree that this particular human life of its 80 or so years is a one-off event. It will never be repeated. And as such, it can be enjoyed to the full, or not.

Encourages appreciation of life

P: So what you seem to be saying is that by appreciating the reality and finality of death, we can be spurred onto a greater appreciation and enjoyment of life.

S: Precisely. And what makes this even more salient and pressing is that we don't know how soon the end of life will come. I don't wish to heap on the morbidity, but death could strike us today. It will strike 150,000 people in the world. One of those people could be us.

And if it's not today, we could be one of tomorrow's 150,000. That's 149,999 plus you or me. In less than 120 years all of us who are now alive will all be dead. Our collective lifetimes will have gone. Memories at best. Now that's not a cause for morbid concern; it's a cause for enlightened change.

P: Is there not a quote about 'the only certain thing in life is death'?

Live in the now

S: Yes, and that being the case, there is no time to wait to start enjoying what remains of our life. To paraphrase something Robin Sharma says in his inspiring book, 'The Monk who sold his Ferrari', '50 years ago may have been the best time for me to start enjoying life. But the next best time is right now'.

It's thinking how you would live today if it was your last day. And then starting to live that life right now. Actually the concept of right now is also helpful in this discussion of recognising we're going to die.

P: What do you mean?

S: 'Being in the now' is a principle used by many groups who appreciate the benefits of gaining more control over the mind. It's a key element of Buddhist thinking and also for those who practice mindfulness and Cognitive Behavioural Therapy (CBT).

The only time to live your life is in the now. There's no point living in the past as the past is past and cannot be changed or relived. There's no point living in the future, because the future is not here, may never be here and is unlikely to ever be here in the form in which we expect or fear it. There's only one time that is here, and that is the now.

P: Is that not a bit short-sighted? Not making plans for the future?

S: It's not saying live for the now, but in the now. It's not saying don't plan for the future or have future objectives. Just don't live there. Don't be living for the next weekend, or for the next holiday, or for when the exams are over, or for when the new car arrives or for your retirement. These events may not come. Even if they do come, they'll probably not be up to the high expectations you had for them.

Vision for the future

P: But what about having some kind of longer term vision for your life? Surely this is important.

S: I completely agree. This is not about drifting aimlessly, being driven by whatever each day brings. Having a clear vision and purpose for our life is important. For some it may be to become a millionaire, or CEO, or run their own business. For others it may be to travel the world, or experience everything life has to offer, or excel in a particular sport or technical field. And for others it may be to have a strong and supportive family life or to be rewarded with some future life. My personal vision is to have a fully enjoyable life by exercising a fit and healthy mind. And my intent is to help others do the same.

Wishing our lives away

P: So it's good to have a vision for the future, but not to be living in that future.

S: Yes. We are often wishing the present to pass so that the next anticipated excitement comes quicker. For the week to pass so we can get to the weekend. For months to pass so we get to holiday time. What a waste of the precious time of our lives. We're spending our lives in existence mode, waiting for the future, rather than enjoying the here and now. And ironically when these highly anticipated events come round they're often below the high expectations we set for them.

P: What do you mean?

S: We're on the dream overseas vacation, but we're still living in future mode. Sitting by the pool, but longing for that special excursion later in the week. On the excursion, but thinking about the special final night dinner. Eating the dinner, but looking forward to the final night party. At the party, but looking forward to getting home and sharing our photos with our friends. Or for a proper British cup of tea!

The past is past

P: But what about the past? Surely there are happy memories to be reflected upon?

S: So reflect on the past. Enjoy bringing to mind the great experiences you have had, together with the learnings. But don't live there. Don't hanker back, wishing you were still living that life. That the children were still young, that your friend was still alive, that you still had that job, or lived in that house or were able to go on that holiday. Don't harbour regrets about the moves you could have made, or the conversations you should or should not have had or the major disagreements which impacted relationships. The more that you hanker back and wish forward, the less you experience the only place where life is, which is the now.

P: That's a really powerful thought. Contrary to what seems right, but I guess a lot of this is.

S: There's sometimes a danger we want to be wherever we are not. If we're at home, we'd rather be abroad; if we're abroad we'd rather be back at home. If we're alone, we'd rather be with others; if we're with others, we'd rather be alone.

P: That's true. So how do you stop it?

S: By saying to yourself, this is where I am. This is where my life is right now. So let me enjoy it to the full in the here and in the now.

P: Anything else you can do to help gain this focus in the present?

S: A motivating way to start each day is an exercise called 'Energise your Intent'. We can look at it later, but basically it helps you to set a positive intent for the day, rather than being negatively influenced by external events. It helps you to fill your mind with all of life's positives and to mentally prepare your mind for the challenges of the day ahead.

P: I guess that's a good way of recognising the value of each day as it comes. And helps to wake us up to the impermanence and transience of life and the need to seize it whilst it's here.

Permanent structures don't make life any more permanent

S: It's strange isn't it? We build permanent structures around us almost as a way of giving ourselves more of a sense of permanence and endurance. We somehow feel less vulnerable to death and more protected from its grasp by surrounding ourselves with more physical and material edifices. But it's delusional. Better to accept we're like sandcastles and snowmen. Temporary and transient.

P: I guess it's also a good way of putting all the petty things which we tend to concern ourselves with into perspective.

S: Yes. How many of us on our deathbed moment will wish the edges of the grass had been trimmed more neatly, or the kids had done the washing up more regularly, or our partner had hung the towels more evenly?!

P: So it seems you can view death in two ways. Either it's something to be feared and so put to the back of your mind, hoping it will never come, and just facing up to it as best you can when it inevitably does. Or you can open your mind to its reality.

Terminal illness effect

S: Yes and whilst not rejoicing in its reality and inevitability, at least using it as a springboard to seize opportunities to enjoy life whilst they're still here. Live a 'last day' life.

The people who get this message most powerfully are those who are diagnosed with a terminal illness at an early age. Steve Jobs is a good case in point. It becomes a real wakeup call for them. To realise that life has a finality and that finality is not far away.

Those are the people who then start living their lives with more of a focus on Enjoy Life. The tragedy is that it took the impending reality of near death to jumpstart the transformation. And the equal tragedy is that we don't all learn from their example and use it to trigger the same transformation in our own lives.

P: I must admit this has been a useful diversion. But can we get back to talking about life again now?!

5. ENJOYMENT V HAPPINESS

S: You mentioned you wanted to start talking about life again. Anything in particular?

P: Yes. Just recap briefly on how you define enjoyment.

S: Enjoyment is always seeing and experiencing the positive of any and every situation. Minimising the negative emotions we all have, like fear, anger, stress and jealousy. Experiencing a constant sense of being at one with yourself and others. Appreciating the power of giving, which leads to even greater levels of enjoyment for yourself and others.

P: So is that any different from the pursuit of happiness?

Enjoyment versus happiness

S: I view happiness as a single emotion. It's more of a temporarily heightened sense of pleasure or joy. It makes you think of a smiley face. It has a lightness and brightness. And whilst it's a great purpose to pursue, it's virtually impossible to sustain that single emotion 24/7. Enjoyment is a broader state of mind and being

P: Can you expand a bit more?

S: If you seek enjoyment, there are indeed occasions when you feel happy. But there are others when you feel enriched or enlightened. Or others when you feel strengthened, invigorated or enthused. Or yet others when you feel free from stress or worry, anger or anxiety, frustration or jealousy. So enjoyment is broader than the single emotion of happiness.

Back to our earlier conversation, I wouldn't expect you to feel happy when your football team loses, but it needn't impact your enjoyment of life. In the same way, I wouldn't expect you to be happy when your children fail their school exams, but again it needn't dent your enjoyment of life. You can still put it into a life context, you can still seek for the positives, you can still find learnings that will help in the future.

P: What about contentment? Do you consider that as different?

Enjoyment versus contentment

S: Contentment is another single emotion. A sense of being at one with oneself and the world. A satisfied state. A fulfilled state. But without the stimulated positivity and mental flexibility that are part of the broader state of enjoyment. If you seek to enjoy life, contentment will be one of the rich tapestry of positive emotions you'll experience.

P: Is this similar to the thinking of some religious

groups?

S: Buddhist teaching focuses on developing a mind of inner peace, one where all emotions are controlled. Through meditation and other spiritual practices, Buddhists seek to eliminate negative, disturbed states of mind and replace them with positive, peaceful states. Buddhism is the calm, serene, tranquil lake approach to mind control.

A mind that seeks enjoyment, however, is one which not only focuses on controlling negative emotions, but also encourages the full experiencing of positive ones. It's more like a flowing river with a gushing waterfall. There's energy and vitality.

P: I guess either scenario is more attractive than the turbulent sea which many people experience in their minds and which I experience from time to time. Highs and lows, strong forces that are difficult to control and take you where you don't want to go, times of feeling swamped and almost drowning.

S: Interesting analogy. So what do you think about it?

P: I understand what you're saying. Enjoyment does seem to have more depth and breadth than those more singular emotional states like happiness and contentment. And I like the fact that it's not about the suppression of positive emotions, but rather the embracing and celebration of them.

I do wonder though how easy it is to apply in practice.

S: Easier than not...

6. EXERCISING A FIT AND HEALTHY MIND

S: So we've spoken quite a lot about having an Enjoyable Life. Why don't we talk about the source, which is a Fit and Healthy Mind? In the same way as we can enjoy the physical aspects of life with a fit and healthy body, so we can enjoy our overall life by exercising a fit and healthy mind.

P: Do you want to expand more on what you mean by a fit and healthy mind?

Fit and healthy mind

S: There are different levels to this, but let's start at the top. It's a mind which, when faced with any situation, is able to respond in a positive, strong, balanced, flexible and emotionally unburdened way.

P: For example?

S: Let's say you're driving to a meeting with your boss and there's a blockage caused by an accident on the road ahead. What's your reaction?

P: I guess one of annoyance and frustration, and probably concern that I'm going to get a hard time from my boss for being late for an important meeting.

S: With a fit and healthy mind, you wouldn't have these negative feelings. They really are pointless, toxic emotions. They're not good for your mind or body, and certainly not for your enjoyment of the day or the moment.

P: But they're natural. That's how everyone would feel.

S: But they don't have to be the emotions and reactions you feel. Back to our discussions about Enjoying Life. The route to an enjoyable life is the choice of how your mind responds to any situation. A Fit and Healthy Mind is one which can respond to this type of situation in a positive, strong, balanced, flexible and emotionally unburdened way.

Putting it into practice

P: So what does that mean in practice?

S: Firstly, putting the situation into context. This is one meeting out of hundreds and however important it may feel at the time, it will not be critical to your overall enjoyment of life. This is not something you will recall on your deathbed and regret. In fact in a few weeks or even days or maybe hours, you'll have forgotten all about it.

Secondly, realising nothing is gained by flooding

the mind with negative emotions. Not only do they make the moment less enjoyable, they also cloud your judgement as to what practical steps you could take in finding an alternative route, finding an alternative means of transport, or explaining to your boss what has happened and discussing alternative options for meeting up.

Thirdly, accepting the external situation and then positively seeking to enjoy the moment.

P: Enjoy being stuck in a traffic jam, late for a meeting?! Are you serious?!

S: You might reflect on the fact that you're not personally involved in the accident. Your health is unaffected, which is a big positive compared to the people in the crashed cars ahead. It's always good to reflect on the relatively good health we have. It's particularly at moments when other people's health is suffering or our own health is not as good as normal, that we are given a powerful prompt to be thankful for the good health we enjoy most of the time.

You could also reflect on the fact that you have a car to get to work. You have a job to go to. Most of the time, you're not stuck in traffic. These are things we tend to take for granted, but most people in the world don't enjoy these positive factors. And they would love to be in your temporarily delayed situation to receive all the other things you have and yet seem to ignore.

Finally, view it that you now have an unexpected opportunity to just sit and reflect. To think through a few things which are on your mind. Or to listen to some music and think of nothing!

P: But is that natural? It's not the way my brain is wired to think.

S: We assume that what comes naturally is good. But that's not necessarily the case. Much of our natural nature is self-seeking. Much of our natural nature has over-stimulated negative responses. We can control our natural responses and develop more positive, more strengthened, more flexible natural responses. This is what exercising a fit and healthy mind is all about.

P: OK, so let's go down to the next level of a fit and healthy mind. You said it linked with the idea of a fit and healthy body.

Five components of physical fitness

S: Yes. There are five components that make up physical fitness. These are:

1. Cardio-vascular fitness
2. Muscular strength
3. Muscular endurance
4. Flexibility
5. Body composition

Cardio-vascular fitness

P: Let's search online and get some more detailed information. The first is cardio-vascular fitness:

Cardio-vascular fitness is the ability of the heart, blood vessels and lungs to pump oxygen-rich blood to the working muscles. This releases energy from foodstuffs and removes toxins and other waste materials from the body. As a result, the body can capably and confidently undertake normal everyday activities. Plus, it's in great shape to face more physically demanding exertions with relative ease.

Positive thinking fitness

S: It's similar with a fit and healthy mind. Cardio-vascular fitness translates into positive thinking fitness:

Positive thinking fitness is the ability of the mind to pump positive-filled thoughts, feelings and emotions around to the different mental muscles. These quickly and powerfully displace and replace any stale negative thoughts, feelings and emotions which have accumulated there. Mental blockages are dislodged and negative toxic thoughts are discharged. As a result, the mind can capably and confidently undertake normal everyday activities. Plus, it's in great shape to face more emotionally demanding exertions with relative ease.

Fitness benefits

P: Cardio-vascular fitness obviously provides you with lots of health benefits. There's less risk of cardio-vascular disease, Type 2 diabetes, blood pressure, strokes, cholesterol problems and obesity. And you boost your body's immune system.

S: It's similar with positive thinking fitness. Your mind is able to operate more freely and positively. It's less clogged with the emotional blockages and baggage that keep negative thoughts circulating around your mind. And your mental immune system is boosted, providing greater resistance and resilience to negative thinking.

Positive thinking fitness exercises

P: Cardio-vascular fitness is obviously developed through aerobic exercises like running and cycling. Are there any exercises to help develop positive thinking fitness?

S: There are a range of exercises which we can look at in detail later. Just to give you a flavour, one of my favourites is called 'Gratitude v Gaptitude'. This involves training our mind to reflect upon what we already have and expressing gratitude for it, rather than focusing on what we don't have (the gap) and experiencing frustration, jealousy or disappointment. Expressing Gratitude automatically pumps more positive thoughts and feelings around our mind.

It's also worth mentioning that there's a link between the physical and mental. Cardio-vascular fitness helps boost our mental mood through the release of endorphins. And when we're in that positive mental state, we're more likely to have the positive intentions and self-determination to undertake physical exercise.

P: So having a fit and healthy mind encourages the development of a fit and healthy body, which in turn further boosts our fit and healthy mind.

S: Exactly. And that's a great basis for enjoying life.

Muscular strength

P: Shall we look at the second component of physical fitness, which is muscular strength?

Muscular strength is the amount of force a muscle

or muscle group can exert against a heavy resistance. It's the ability of the body to lift a heavy weight.

Mental strength

S: Linking it to the mind, we can conceive of mental muscles and mental strength:

Mental strength is the ability of our mind to handle heavy mental pressures and forces. It's about mental strength in the face of emotional challenge.

P: So how might you use this concept of mental strength?

S: Think about all the different emotional challenges you face throughout the day. It may be your boss doing something which you find annoying, it may be having to present to a group, it may be your partner saying something which you view as upsetting, it may be the children doing something which you find worrying, it may be someone taking a long time in a queue which you find frustrating, it may be a comment from a neighbour which makes you feel jealous, it may be an article in a newspaper which you interpret as distressing etc.

P: So where does mental strength come in?

S: This is what enables you to resist converting them into negative emotions, by seeing them for what they are. External stimuli, to which you have the mental strength to respond in a strong, balanced, centred and composed way. Not allowing these external pressures to deal you an emotional blow. Not letting them knock you off your positive mental course of enjoying life. Not letting the weight win.

P: But what about more traumatic events like losing your job or being diagnosed with a terminal illness or experiencing the death of a close friend or family member?

S: These are obviously heavy pressures to bear. And they are bound to hit you hard. But the point about building mental strength is that you will be better prepared to handle the hard emotional hits. You will still be emotionally touched, bruised and damaged. There is obviously a huge gap between the mental strength required to overcome feelings of anxiety before an exam and overcoming the upset from the loss of a loved one. But, and this is the important point, the more you have built your mental muscle strength in the everyday challenges, the better mental condition you will be in to handle the real hard emotional blows when they come.

Mental strength exercises

P: So are there exercises to help develop mental strength as there are for physical muscular strength?

S: Absolutely. You can view all of life as a mental gym for the mind. Every daily challenge is an opportunity to develop stronger mental muscles.

P: In the gym there are exercises for building up different muscle groups like quads, pecs and abs. You start with low weights and resistance and gradually build up to more intense levels.

S: It's exactly the same principle with your mind. You start with emotional pressures that your mental muscles can manage with a little effort. It may be that you don't feel comfortable going to new places and meeting new people. So start with a low pressure environment, maybe going to a familiar place along with your partner or close friend and meeting new people there. When you're comfortable with that, build up the intensity and try going with your partner or friend to a completely new place and mixing with people there. And when you've developed the mental strength for that, step out and go on your own to a new place and meet up with totally new people.

P: It says that different people have different physical muscle strengths and weaknesses and so have different focus areas to work on and develop.

S: Same again with the mind. One person may have a strong and developed mental muscle group for handling high pressure work situations. But they may have weak mental muscles when it comes to feelings of jealousy and struggle to handle other people's success. Another person may have strong mental muscles in handling their children's misbehaviour, but may not be so strong at handling events which don't work out as planned or in having the social confidence to meet new people.

P: I suppose the good news is that unlike a physical gym, the mental gym is always there.

S: Yes. And you can decide when, what and how you want to exercise. You may decide one particular week that you want to strengthen a mental muscle group dealing with factors which normally induce anger within you. You could start practicing with the easier emotional weights and pressures, things that have previously caused minor irritation. Then gradually build up to the heavier weights and pressures, those

47

factors that would previously have caused strong feelings of anger.

P: In the gym, you can always have a go with a really heavy weight to see whether you can lift it at all. And if not, set yourself a goal of being able to manage it by a certain date.

S: Same with the mind. Take that person, situation or activity that you find hardest to manage. Try dealing with it. See how you do. And if you can't manage it at this stage, set that as your goal.

P: And you're suggesting this will help manage the tougher emotional challenges like suffering from a serious injury, terminal illness or the death of a loved one?

S: Definitely. And to put a sobering context to this, if you find you're using words such as catastrophe, crisis, disaster and nightmare to describe what happens when a glass gets knocked over or a soufflé doesn't rise, you're going to be in serious mental trouble when a real cause for concern arises!

P: Seems sound. And I like the way that what I'd previously considered as emotional problems are now framed as mental challenges. So you start to view them in a positive way, using them as an opportunity to build up your mental muscle strength and develop a fitter and healthier mind.

Shall we look at the third component of physical fitness, which is muscular endurance?

Muscular endurance

S: Yes. How is that defined?

P: It says:

Muscular endurance is the ability of a muscle or muscle group to repeat a movement many times or to hold a particular position for an extended period of time. It's resilience in the face of repetitions of a constant weight or pressure. It's the ability to lift a small to medium weight a large number of times. Or in running terms, it's the ability to run a marathon.

Mental endurance

S: The parallel is mental endurance.

Mental endurance is the ability of our mind to sustain constant emotional pressure. It's mental resilience. It's being able to positively withstand regular emotional pressures and challenges. Not letting the weight win.

P: For instance?

S: At work, it may be the ability to withstand the constant bad-temperedness of your boss. At home, it may be handling the constant moaning of the children. With a partner, it may be handling their constant nagging or bad moods.

Mental endurance exercises

P: To develop muscular endurance, you select the maximum weight you can lift 12-20 times. Then you repeat the exercise a number of times. What about mental endurance?

S: It's similar. Choose an emotional pressure which is not too intense. It could be the children constantly arguing. Maybe you normally fly off the handle the third time in the day that they argue. Try extending that to the fifth time, then the tenth time and so on until you have developed a mental resilience that can handle it virtually every time. Or it could have been the third nag from your partner that set your blood boiling. Try to extend it to the sixth comment and then the tenth comment and see whether you can build up a mental resilience that can take all these comments (previously considered as nags!) without generating a negative response.

P: You know with physical muscle memory, once your muscles have completed a particular movement a number of times, it becomes instinctive behaviour? Does the same apply to the mental muscles?

S: Yes. By regularly working out your mental muscles, you're able to build up their strength and resilience because they remember the previous times a similar situation arose and start to naturally respond in the same way. There is a whole field of psychological research on this topic, which is termed neuroplasticity.

If, for example, you've trained your mental muscles not to get frustrated when you're behind a Learner Driver and have repeated it the last 4 or 5 times, it will then become an instinctive reaction. You won't need to think about responding in a positive, non-frustrated way. Your mind just will. Then you're beginning to make serious progress!

And bear in mind this is not mental exercise for its own sake. It's the route to living a more enjoyable life.

Remember it's about enjoying life

P: I'm pleased you said that. It was potentially starting to feel a bit like hard work!

S: All these exercises are linked to the overall intent of enjoying life. The route is through a fit and healthy mind. This is the part we're now focusing on, but it's always with the 'enjoy life' goal in mind. None of this should involve periods of unenjoyment, if that's a word?!

P: It is now!

S: Shall we move onto the fourth component of physical fitness, which is flexibility?

Flexibility

P: It says:

Flexibility is the ability of the body to fluidly stretch and extend. It's also about physical poise, control, balance and stability.

Mental flexibility

S: It's easy to see how that parallels directly with a fit and healthy mind:

Mental flexibility means your mind is no longer tight, rigid and inflexible. Rather, it has a fluidity flexibility and adaptability, able to reach many alternative options and possible solutions. It is able to retain its poise, control, balance and stability in the face of many different pressures and challenges. It is centred and grounded, but enjoys free and fluid movement and versatility.

P: And how might you use that mental flexibility?

S: Just think about all those times when you've felt angered, stressed or upset because of the inflexibility of your thinking. You wanted it to be done a certain way and it was done in a different way. You expected to receive something by a certain time and it came later. You resolutely followed one particular route to solving a problem, believing it to be the only one, to find that someone had tried an alternative approach and had come up with a much better solution. You stuck to your guns on an issue and ended up being shot down for it. You thought your children would only succeed if they followed a particular route of your conceiving and they rebelled against it and went an alternative route, which actually turned out better. And so on…

P: OK, but is a flexible mind not a sign of weakness? If you're always seeing things from other people's points of view and letting them have their way?

S: It's important not to confuse flexibility with fragility. Or suppleness with submissiveness. It's actually quite the reverse. Mental flexibility is a sign of a truly fit and healthy mind. It is mental rigidity that is actually weakness, albeit masquerading as strength.

Mental flexibility exercises

P: And can you exercise the mind to develop mental flexibility?

S: Again, it makes sense to start with the easier stretches and movements. As with the body, the areas where we have less flexibility vary by individual. Your's may be around time, where you never allow any latitude for people to be late. So you could try to be more flexible around the meeting of deadlines. Start with some unimportant ones first. See whether it actually leads to a better atmosphere and maybe even a better result. Then move to some more critical ones. And when you feel you really want a test of your time flexibility, try going to Indonesia and set some time deadlines there. They actually have an expression to reflect their time flexibility (a polite term for always being late!), which is 'jam karet', meaning 'rubber time'!

P: Any other examples?

S: Your mind may be less flexible in coming up with alternative solutions to a challenge. Try to develop your mental suppleness in this area. Start with something easy like varying your food choices, or morning routines, or coming up with alternative activities for when the weather is different to what you expected. Then gradually stretch to more challenging situations, people and activities. And don't forget to do it with the positive intention of living a more enjoyable life.

P: This is something I'm looking forward to trying. If I'm honest, I am a little rigid and inflexible in my thinking. I'd considered it a virtue of knowing my mind, but now I'm beginning to see it slightly differently. I do tend to shy away from options that I don't feel comfortable with, which does limit possibilities and restricts my ability to understand other people's perspectives.

Body composition

S: So while you're mulling that over, are you ready to look at the fifth and final component of physical fitness, which is body composition?

P: *Body composition is described as:*

> *the proportion of lean tissues (muscle, bones and organs) that are metabolically active, compared to fat tissue, which is not. It's the distinction between body mass which is helpful in producing substances and energy that are required to sustain life, and that which is not. Muscles give us the energy and ability to lead an active physical life, whereas excess fat slows us down, restricts our physical movement and causes us to suffer problems like heart disease and Type 2 diabetes.*

Mind composition

S: From a fit and healthy mind perspective, this translates into mind composition.

> *Mind composition is the proportion of lean mental muscle compared to mental fat. Lean mental muscles are the generators of positive thoughts, feelings and emotions. They are full of positive energy, strength, endurance and flexibility. Mental fat harbours and oozes negative thoughts, feelings and emotions. It saps positive energy. It is obstructive and restrictive and clogs the arteries of the mind. And as a result leads to unhealthy thinking.*

P: So how would you look to improve your mind composition? How would you increase the ratio of lean mental muscle to mental fat?

Mind composition exercises

S: As with physical fitness, there are two methods. One is exercise and the other is diet.

P: Starting with exercise, it says here that physical body composition is impacted by the other four components of physical fitness. The body's lean to fat tissue ratio can be improved through exercises in cardio-vascular, muscular strength, muscular endurance and flexibility. Is it similar with mind composition?

S: Yes. There are exercises we can discuss later for enhancing positive thinking, mental strength, mental endurance and mental flexibility. They all contribute to building the lean muscles of the mind and burning off the mental fat. They work in combination to oxygenate the mind with positive thoughts, build and strengthen the mental muscles and develop mental flexibility.

P: What about diet?

Mental diet

S: Again it's similar to physical diet. In the same way that you are what you eat, your mind is what you mentally digest.

P: With physical diet, it's a matter of consuming what your body can comfortably manage, depending on its level of health and fitness. Calorie intake needs to take account of the body's metabolism and its activity levels, which determine how much energy it will burn. We need to watch our intake of fats, salt and sugar. What about diet for the mind?

S: It's a matter of consuming what your mind can comfortably manage, depending on its level of health and fitness. It's not about leading the life of a recluse and cutting yourself off from the world. This runs the risk of becoming mentally anorexic, lacking the strength to face any challenge. But neither is it about throwing yourself into every emotionally charged situation believing you can mentally cope with it. This runs the risk of becoming mentally obese.

P: Are you suggesting it varies by individual?

S: Everyone needs to watch their mental diet, but the right intake levels do vary by individual. If you already have a pretty fit and healthy mind, you'll be able to manage a higher mental calorific load. You'll be able to cope more easily with the highly charged emotional energies of living with rebellious teenage children or of a high pressured job. You'll be able to turn this stimulation into stronger and more resilient mental muscles. But for others, this high octane intake will simply result in the accumulation of more fatty thinking and greater mental fat deposits.

P: So is it just the emotionally energised situations people need to carefully manage?

S: I guess you could stretch the analogy to also watch out for the over salty, oversweet and bad fat types if you really wanted to!

P: Go on.

S: You know the over salty types. Those who have stinging outbursts of anger, jealousy and stress which can easily raise the pressure levels in our minds.

P: And the oversweet ones?

S: Those who are loaded with sweet saccharin praise that can cause unhealthy ego-loaded rushes of blood to the head.

P: And the bad fat ones?

S: Those who are saturated with negativity. They ooze unhealthy thoughts. They are laden with criticism and cynicism. They're like stodgy doughnuts with a hollow centre of disappointment. Again, if you have a fit and healthy mind you're better able to absorb these inputs. But for many, they simply contribute to the build up of fatty mental deposits.

P: As you say, a little overstretch of the analogy, but it does build up some interesting pictures in your mind of what to avoid or cut back on!

S: So we've explored the five components of a fit and healthy mind. What do you think?

P: Very interesting concept. Can we just map out the five components of physical fitness and a fit and healthy mind side by side? That will provide a useful quick reference of how they relate.

Component of Physical Fitness	Brief Description	Component of Fit & Healthy Mind	Brief Description
Cardio-vascular Fitness	Ability of heart, blood vessels and lungs to pump oxygen-rich blood to the working muscles.	Positive Thinking Fitness	Ability of the mind to pump positive-filled thoughts, feelings and emotions around to the different mental muscles.
Muscular Strength	Amount of force a muscle or muscle group can exert against a heavy resistance.	Mental Strength	Ability of the mind to handle heavy mental pressures and forces. Mental strength in the face of emotional challenge.
Muscular Endurance	Ability of a muscle or muscle group to repeat a movement many times or to hold a particular position for an extended period of time.	Mental Endurance	Ability of the mind to withstand constant emotional pressure. Mental resilience.

Flexibility	Ability of the body to fluidly stretch and reach. Physical poise, control, balance and stability.	Mental Flexibility	Ability of the mind to act with fluidity, flexibility and adaptability to reach many different options and solutions. Ability to retain mental poise, control, balance and stability.
Body Composition	Proportion of lean tissues (muscle, bones and organs) that are metabolically active, compared to fat tissue, which is not.	Mind Composition	Proportion of lean mental muscle to mental fat. Lean mental muscles generate positive thoughts, feelings and emotions. Mental fat harbours and oozes negative thoughts, feelings and emotions.

7. EXERCISES FOR ENJOYING LIFE

7.1. Energise your Intent

P: You mentioned there's a useful exercise to start each day.

S: This is one I've developed called 'Energise your Intent'. It's about setting a positive intent for the day. So instead of allowing the external events of the day to dictate your enjoyment, you set out with your clear intent to enjoy the day, come what may. You energise yourself to achieve enjoyment from your internal resource and response, rather than any external event. It's an effective way of warming up all the components of a fit and healthy mind. It's similar to the practice many religious people have of starting each day with meditation or prayer and so elevating their thinking to a more spiritual plane.

P: How do you do it?

S: Before getting out of bed, I just take a few minutes of reflection and intent setting. I always begin by being grateful for my life. For the opportunity to wake up to another day, recognising that many won't. And one day, nor will I. I also express gratitude for the lives of those who mean a lot to me, my family and close friends. I express my gratitude for my health - that I can still do virtually anything I want. And even if I'm feeling a bit under the weather or have some minor illness, I still reflect positively about the overall health that I do have, considering how so many people are incapacitated in various ways.

Start with gratitude

P: So you start the day with a sense of gratitude.

S: Yes. I think this is really important. We can look at another exercise later which is based on the difference between what I've termed Gratitude and Gaptitude. Unfortunately, we often express Gaptitude rather than Gratitude, focusing on what we don't have rather than the many things we do. And this is one of the primary causes of our unenjoyment of life.

P: Is there anything else you express gratitude for?

S: The opportunity to live in a country where we have freedom and live in relative safety. The comfort of my home and the opportunity to spend the day doing things that can give me enjoyment.

P: How else do you energise your positive intent?

Every day is a one-off

S: I frame the significance of the day by realising that this is the only 15th of February 2012 (or whatever date it is) which will ever be. Within less than 24 hours it will be over. The sun has risen, the sun will set, the rest is up to me. This is a day where I have the opportunity to enjoy life. I'm going to positively enjoy the 15th of February 2012. In fact I'm going to enjoy each hour of this day. Starting now.

Whatever lies ahead, whether it's a challenging day at work, a day walking in the hills or a day relaxing with friends, I'll think positively about what enjoyment that can bring. I'll also set an intent to use my fit and healthy mind to experience everything in a positive way, to use the strength and endurance in my mental muscles to handle any emotional challenges, to consider things in a flexible way and to develop more lean thinking and burn up more negative emotional fat.

P: Anything else?

S: It depends on the day. Sometimes if I know I have a particular emotional challenge coming up, I'll focus on how I can treat it as an opportunity to build up a particular set of mental muscles. Or if I wake up having had a poor night's sleep, because certain negative thoughts kept circulating in my mind, I'll also run through a quick 'Un-CLOG your Mind' drill or 'Ill at Es to Healthy Ps' routine. We can talk about those exercises a little later as well.

P: So does this work? Does this actually set you up for a perfect day of enjoyment?

Mindset shapes events

S: It's not a guarantee of a utopian day! But I know that when I don't do it, the day's events start to impact my mindset, rather than my mindset impacting the way I view them.

You know that classic start to the day when you open the curtains, look at the weather and say 'it's a bad day'. How unhelpful is that. It's not a bad day. There's just a certain kind of weather occurring outside. That doesn't make it a bad day. The only reason it might be a bad day is we've chosen to view it that way, with the weather being an external stimulus. And if you want to view life that way, that's OK. But since the weather in England is what people term as 'bad' a lot of the time, a lot of people are going to have a lot of 'bad days'!

P: Are there any other examples where external factors may previously have impacted your enjoyment at the start of the day?

S: I may have been annoyed that it's wet and windy outside which will make my daily jog less pleasant. Or I may have been frustrated that the printer is playing up again. Or I've been troubled by too many emails coming in during the night. Or I've been troubled with not enough emails coming in during the night! Or I've been niggled that my mother-in-law has rung just as we're about to have breakfast. Or I've been cross that my son has once again left the TV remote control stuffed down the side of the seat cushion.

P: Maybe that's because you're a naturally grumpy person?!

S: Maybe you're right! As I said when we started this conversation, I'm not a shining light who epitomises enjoyment every moment of every day. I'm just a human being who has a desire and intent to live a more enjoyable life. By exercising a fit and healthy mind in this way I find I can.

Assessing progress

P: So how do you assess your progress?

S: Interesting question. This whole approach is based on having yourself as your own benchmark. It's not about trying to have a more enjoyable life than someone else. The moment it becomes competitive, you've lost. There's only one comparison point and that is yourself and your own enjoyment. Am I enjoying my life? Am I enjoying my life more than before?

If not, there's no need to beat yourself up about it. Just reconsider, refocus and give it another go. And if you're anything like me, you'll find that apart from the odd down day, you'll definitely have a greater overall level of enjoyment as your mind becomes fitter and healthier. Also, as your positivity is noticed by others, and starts to influence their thinking and behaviour, you'll find you benefit from their more positive outlook and interaction.

P: Is 'Energise your Intent' something you only do at the start of the day?

S: It's certainly the best way to start a day, but then I'll regularly re-energise my intent as the day progresses. Not in a dutiful or over-systemised way. But it starts to become second nature to regularly reflect on whether I'm enjoying the moment. If I am, then I'll reflect on why and be grateful. If not, I'll try to understand why not, and do a quick mind fitness exercise to re-energise my enjoyment.

P: It sounds a really inspiring approach. Certainly not time consuming and if it provides the opportunity to get more enjoyment from each day, it's probably worth giving it a try.

Give it a go

Why not start tomorrow morning by 'Energising your Intent'?

- Take around 5 minutes before you get out of bed.
- Start by expressing gratitude. Reflect on everything you have - your life, health, family, friends and any and everything else. And be grateful. This will start to fill your mind with positive thoughts.
- Recognise that this day is a one-off opportunity. It will never be repeated and it may be your last. So commit to yourself that you are going to enjoy it. Fully. Starting now.
- Commit to exercising your mental muscles during the day. To be both strong and resilient in the face of all emotional pressures.
- Set an intent to be flexible in your thinking, to be more adaptable and open to different thoughts, ideas and approaches. And to retain mental balance and poise as you face the challenges and opportunities of the day ahead.
- Commit to using the day to build up more lean mental muscle and burn off any unhelpful mental fat.
- And finally, just before you get out of bed, say to yourself: 'I am going to enjoy this day, to the full, starting right now'.

Tips

- Remember it's worth the time investment. You may well think this is 5 minutes when you could be getting up and on with the day ahead. But it's the critical 5 minutes which will shape whether and how you enjoy the whole day ahead.
- Ensure you keep your reflections fresh and relevant for each day, rather than performing the exercise in rote fashion.
- On occasions, energise your intent with others, which will give both you and them an extra energising boost.

7.2. Gratitude v Gaptitude

S: I mentioned earlier that a useful exercise is to express Gratitude rather than Gaptitude. Gratitude is focusing on what we have and experiencing a sense of appreciation. What I've termed 'Gaptitude' is focusing on what we don't have and experiencing a sense of resentment, jealousy, frustration, yearning or disappointment. This is a great exercise for boosting Positive Thinking Fitness.

P: But it's natural to focus on what we don't yet have. That's what drive and ambition are all about. That's how we progress.

Drive and ambition

S: I'm not suggesting there's anything wrong with having drive and ambition. But for what? What is it we're trying to achieve? More material things? A bigger house? More longhaul holidays? A higher salary? For what ultimate purpose? To enjoy life more? But as we've discussed at length already, this is not where real enjoyment comes from.

P: So why bother having drive and ambition?

S: To drive towards a more genuinely enjoyable life. This is a meaningful and worthwhile ambition.

P: So how does the Gratitude v Gaptitude thing come in?

S: It recognises there will always be a gap between what we have and what we want. As soon as we get the thing we've been craving, we immediately set our sights on our next craving. So we have a choice. We can keep focusing on what's missing or focus on what we already have.

P: But if we focus on what's missing, we can get it and then become more satisfied.

S: That's the fallacy. The reality is there will always be something missing. Because for everything we get, there will be the next level we then seek to attain. It's a never ending cycle. If you've got £500k, you'll want £1m. When you've got £1m, you'll want £2m. When you've got a 3-bedroom house, you'll want a 4-bedroom house. When you've got a 4-bedroom house, you'll want a 5-bedroom house. And later in life, when you may have got your 5-bedroom house, you'll want to size back down to a 3-bedroom house!

P: And convince yourself it was all done for good practical reasons! So what's the exercise that can help?

Focus on what you already have

S: It's a simple one of expressing Gratitude not Gaptitude. It's focusing on what you already have, rather than taking that for granted and focusing upon what you don't. It's a mental exercise of reflecting on all the things you already have - family, friends, health, freedom, a house, a car, a job and leisure activities. In fact more than you actually need to lead a fully enjoyable life.

P: And when would you use it?

S: As we said earlier, it's useful as part of 'Energising your Intent'. It's also one you can easily practice any time of the day. So next time you find yourself feeling negative emotions prompted by a sense of yearning for something you don't have or can't have, treat that as a positive stimulus to reflect positively on what you do already have, and look to enjoy life by being content with that.

P: Are there any other times you could use it?

Gratitude at times of loss

S: It's also useful when we lose what we do have. Whenever something that we take for granted goes wrong we tend to become irritated. The printer breaking down, the computer crashing, the bin collector not taking all the rubbish, the newspaper boy delivering the wrong newspaper, road works on the motorway, mislaying our house key. We're expressing Gaptitude, but this time the gap is between what we normally have and what is now missing. But again, if we want to enjoy life by exercising a fit and healthy mind, this is an opportunity to express Gratitude. To reflect and be grateful that most of the time the printer does work, the computer operates, the bin collector takes away all our rubbish, the paper boy delivers the correct newspaper, the motorway is clear and we have our house key.

P: Is this realistic?

S: If you want it to be.

P: But it doesn't help get the problem fixed.

S: Actually it does. Because it means we approach it with a much calmer and more rational mindset. It also means we're able to engage the help of others, rather than flying off the handle and setting up unnecessary barriers.

As we mentioned earlier, a fit and healthy mind approach is not at all about resigned acceptance. It's about responding to every situation in a positive way and through that being able to resolve matters more effectively.

P: It seems counter-intuitive.

S: That might make it right!

P: I'm *grateful* for that thought!

Give it a go

Why not do a quick Gratitude v Gaptitude check right now?

- Take a few minutes to reflect on what has been occupying your mind so far today.
- Create 2 columns, headed Gratitude and Gaptitude. Jot down your thoughts into the respective columns.
- How balanced are the columns? How much more is there in the Gaptitude column?
- For each item in the Gaptitude column, write down 5 related things in the Gratitude column for which you can be grateful.
- For example, if you put 'lots of traffic getting to work' under Gaptitude, you could put in the Gratitude column:
  - Normally a lot less traffic
  - I don't have the 2-hour daily journey that many commuters have
  - I got to work safely
  - I heard an interesting news item on the radio
  - I found an alternative route to work which will save me 5 minutes on other days
- Read through all the items now in the Gratitude column.
- Reflect on how that feels. How you feel so much better about life and are able to put the little difficulties and inconveniences into their rightful context. A weight has lifted off your mind. You are thinking more clearly and positively. You are able to act more clearly and positively. You are enjoying life more.

Tips

- Whenever you're feeling that the world owes you something, use the exercise. It will make you realise how much you already have.
- Remember, the world owes you nothing. You just owe yourself the sense of gratitude to realise what you have.

7.3. Ill at Es to Healthy Ps

S: One of the most helpful exercises is called: 'Ill at Es to Healthy Ps'. You can use this any time you're feeling worried, upset, pressurised, unneeded, jealous, irritated, angry or any other negative emotion. It helps unlock the cause of your negativity and redirect you to a more positive path. I've developed it as a way of exercising all the components of a fit and healthy mind.

P: What do you mean by Ill at Es?

3Es – Ego, Expectation and Emotion(-ve)

S: It's a play on the phrase 'ill at ease'. There are 3Es: Ego, Expectation and Emotion(-ve). It is the combination of these 3Es that often puts us in an unhealthy state of mind.

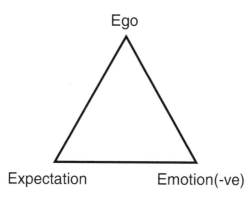

P: Can we talk it through using the scenario of being late for the boss because of the road accident?

S: It's an interesting example of where the thoughts

that dominate our mind are Ego-centred, Expectation-driven and Emotionally-charged. Let's look at how each of them plays out:

Ego – the primary person whose situation is being considered here is *me*. *I* will now be late. *I* have been inconvenienced by this situation. *My* day is ruined. *My* career will be negatively affected.

Expectation – the reason I'm having negative emotions is because I had set *expectations* in my mind which are not being fulfilled. I had *expected* to get to the office by 8.30. I had *expected* to be able to meet my boss. I had *expected* to be able to talk him through my progress on the project. I had *expected* to get his endorsement for the hard work I'd been putting in. I had *expected* to be able to move onto a different project by the end of the week.

Emotion(-ve) – the negative emotions welling up inside me are frustration, irritation towards the person who has caused the accident, disappointment that my boss won't give me the positive endorsement I was seeking and anxiety that my colleague who was also attending the meeting will look more impressive in my boss's eyes.

P: That's a pretty accurate description of how I was feeling. But what's the alternative?

S: If we exercise a fit and healthy mind we can move from Ill at Es to Healthy Ps. These are an antidote to the 3Es. The 3Ps are People, Perspective and Positive thinking.

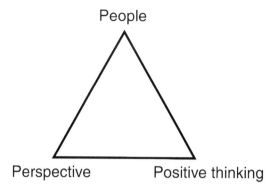

People

Perspective   Positive thinking

So again, applying it to the accident scenario:

People – instead of just focusing on the Ego (me, I, self), think about other people. The people who are actually involved in the accident and may miss more than just a meeting. Other people who have been held up by the accident, some of whom may be missing far more important things.

Perspective – this is a useful antidote to Expectation. Get the whole situation into perspective. Will this missed meeting matter in a week, month or year? Will your boss really think so negatively about you because of a single unavoidable situation that could happen to anyone? How serious a situation is this compared with losing your job, losing your life or losing a loved one?

Positive thinking – fill your mind with the positives of the situation to eradicate the negative thoughts. You're not injured. Your car is not damaged. You're still able to have a meeting with your boss, albeit at a different time, when actually he may be in a better state of mind to go through your project. At least you have a job. You've done some great work so far on the project which is why you were looking forward to sharing it with him. Being stuck in the car for an hour gives you some more time to think through how best to present it. And the clarity of thinking may help you in finding an alternative route or method of getting to work so you may in fact not be too late for the meeting.

'Ill at Es to Healthy Ps' scenario

P: Interesting technique. Let's take another situation. How about something that has really frustrated me recently, which is tearing the cruciate ligament in my knee and not being able to play sport for a couple of months.

S: You talk it through, starting by framing it in terms of being Ill at Es.

P: OK.
    Ego – I guess I've focused heavily on *myself* here with *my* condition, *my* pain, *my* frustration.
    Expectation – I always *expected* to be able to play tennis and go for a run whenever I wanted. It's part of my weekly routine, which I just *expected* to go on happening.
    Emotion(-ve) – I guess that's obvious. I'm feeling pretty frustrated and disappointed about it.

S: Good. Not good that you've injured yourself and are feeling frustrated! But good that you're able to easily use the technique to frame it. Now translate it into Healthy Ps.

P: People – there are other people who are in a much worse condition than me. Many have totally lost the movement in their legs. They would give anything to only have a temporarily torn cruciate ligament and the relative slight inconvenience this causes.
    Perspective – at least it's only my knee and nothing more serious. I've enjoyed playing sport

without any trouble for decades, so a short layoff is not the end of the world. Plus there are lots of other things I can do with the spare time, maybe trying a few different hobbies.

Positive thinking – I can be grateful that I enjoy a pretty healthy life overall. The rest of my body is functioning well. This minor injury is a stimulus to appreciating my general good health and encouraging me to make the most of it whilst I can.

S: As you can see, it's an easy exercise to use and is really powerful in rapidly shifting our mindset from unhealthy negativity to healthy positivity. A particularly helpful thought around keeping a sense of Perspective is a comment a friend's husband quotes when she's complaining about the stresses and strains of her working day. He simply says: 'So on a score of 1-10, where 10 equals death, how serious is it?' That instantly helps her realise that she's allowing her mind to be caught up in ego-driven expectations and emotions that really are not that important.

Ego centred

P: Talking this through has just made me realise how innate and pervasive our ego thinking is. Maybe that's to be expected and it's part of our survival instinct. But it really does lead us to look at life in a very jaundiced way. And since everyone is doing the same, each being led by their own egos, it's no wonder there is so much interpersonal tension and conflict.

S: It's so instinctive we don't even realise we're doing it. It's only when it's pointed out that our ego is dominating virtually all our thoughts that we step back and realise what's happening. That's not to say we should completely lose self and become submissive to the egos of others. But there is scope to de-egotise our thinking. To use Americanised phraseology, we need 'Ego to go!' And ironically, the biggest beneficiary of less self-centred thinking will be our self!

P: Say that again.

S: Contrary to what we might expect, ego elevation is the cause of so much of our lack of enjoyment of life. By putting ego (our views, our needs, our wishes) on a constant pedestal we keep getting it knocked, bruised and damaged. But if we de-egotise ourselves, and think about others as well as ourselves, this will ironically lead to more self-enjoyment.

Expectation driven

P: What about the second E, Expectation?

S: Expectation is also a big impediment to our living an enjoyable life. It's like ego in the sense that we don't realise how pervasive it is. If someone were to ask us for our expectations of the day or an event, we might struggle to think of any. But they're at work in the background of our minds all the time.

P: Do you want to expand?

S: We're affected by three types of expectations:
Expectations relating to ourselves. I expect to be able to achieve this task, hit this deadline, reach this salary level, cook this meal, cycle this distance, have this physical appearance, attract this partner, win this game.
Expectations relating to other people. I expect her to behave this way. I expect him to help me cook the dinner. I expect them to listen to what I'm saying. I

expect you to agree with my point of view.

Expectations relating to events. I expect it to be a sunny day. I expect it will be a great football match. I expect we'll have a great celebration. I expect it will be the holiday of a lifetime.

P: That's a lot of expectations. More than I expected!!

S: What makes it worse is that the expectations relating to ourselves are sometimes magnified into triple expectations. We expect the meal we prepare to be perfect, because we expect that other people will expect it of us!

P: 'Great Expectations' you might say!

Expectation drives disappointment

S: Exactly! And since we don't always use the term 'expect' to precede the thought or statement, we don't realise how much our life is wrapped up in expectation wishes. No wonder we don't enjoy life to the full. We're setting such a high expectation that we're setting ourselves up for regular tension and disappointment.

P: You're right. So many of our feelings relate to a disappointment with what turned out compared to what we expected. I was disappointed with how I performed in the test. She let me down. It wasn't as good a meal as I'd expected. The weather was a disappointment.

S: That last one is quite funny. How can the weather be a disappointment?! The weather is what the weather is. The sun and rain don't conspire to create deliberate disappointment. They just are. The fact that we choose to respond to independent external events and term them a disappointment shows how so much of our lack of enjoyment is fuelled by our own internal expectation setting, driven by our own ego.

P: I hear what you're saying, but surely setting expectations is important if we want to develop and progress. Otherwise our lives become stuck in status quo and inertia.

Intention v Expectation

S: I think it's important to distinguish between intention and expectation. Having intentions is definitely a positive trait to cultivate. It may be an intention to win at a particular sport, or an intention to perform well in an exam or an intention to prepare a delicious meal.

P: So how does that differ from expectation?

S: An intention is a course of action we propose to follow. With intention, we are setting the directional goal. If the intention is not achieved, it's not an emotional letdown. We will have received enjoyment from having set a challenge and made some positive progress, whilst learning from the experience. But with expectation, we set the standard and become emotionally attached to it. If the expectation is not achieved, it becomes a problem. We suffer a sense of disappointment and failure.

P: So why do we set expectations when they so often lead to frustration and disappointment?

S: It's back to our friend Ego again. It's because our Ego says this is how the world should be. This is how I should be. This is how you should be. This is how it should be. That's my expectation of each of you. Now deliver and don't dare let me down!

P: Ego as autocratic dictator.

S: Yes, but a frustrated one, since there are 7 billion other autocratic dictators trying to compete out there!

P: So how does this all link with developing a fit and healthy mind?

Link to fit and healthy mind

S: 'Ill at Es to Healthy Ps' draws on the five components of a fit and healthy mind. It exercises Positive Thinking Fitness to pump positive-filled thoughts, feelings and emotions to displace the negative ones ensconced in the muscles of our mind. It levers Mental Strength and Endurance to counter-resist the forces of Ego and Expectation. It taps into Mental Flexibility, considering other People rather than just ourselves and putting things into Perspective. And finally, it becomes easier the more our Mind Composition is weighted towards lean mental muscle rather than mental fat.

P: So do you need a fit and healthy mind to practice it?

S: It's like all these exercises. The fitter and healthier your mind, the easier it is to perform them. But the way to build a fit and healthy mind is to start exercising.

P: I might just give it a go!

Give it a go

Next time you're feeling really negative about something, try an 'Ill at Es to Healthy Ps' exercise.

- Think about the negative emotion you're feeling. It might be anger, frustration, jealousy, stress, worry, upset etc.
- Reflect on how important your Ego is in the scenario. To what extent is this driven by you, your needs, your desires, your hopes, your perspectives?
- Think about Expectation. What were you expecting? What were you expecting of yourself? What were you expecting of others?
- Think again about the negative Emotion you're feeling. To what extent is this being driven by events not meeting your own Ego-driven Expectations?
- Then switch to a Healthy Ps mindset.
- Think about other People. How bad is your situation compared with others at this moment? Would this be considered so drastic by someone who has just been diagnosed with a terminal illness, just lost their job, just lost their home, just lost a loved one?
- Put the situation into Perspective. Is it really that bad? Remember the 1-10 scale, where 10 equals death. What does it score?
- Having put your Ego-driven Expectations into a broader People Perspective, fill your mind with the Positives of the situation. What are all the things you have and can feel positive about?
- With that clearer, more positive and more balanced mindset, think through any decisions and actions that will help improve the way you are feeling.
- Now get on with enjoying life!

Tips

- Remember this is not about letting your Ego be downtrodden by other People. It's about getting the right Perspective to help put your Ego-driven Expectation in its rightful place.
- Be sensitive to when others are Ill at Es. Use the technique in a positive and kind way to help them reach Healthy Ps.

7.4. STOP Thinking

S: Another technique which evolved as I looked to change my approach to life was 'STOP Thinking'. It's a quick 4-step exercise you can use whenever negative thoughts and feelings are dominating your mind. It exercises all 5 components of a fit and healthy mind.

P: Talk me through it.

STOP

S: The S of STOP also stands for Stop! This is to emphasise this crucial first step, without which nothing will change. When you realise that what you're saying, thinking or feeling is negative, just stop. Stop what you're doing, stop what you're saying, stop what you're thinking.

P: Then what?

S: T is for Time-out. Take a minute or two out and just reflect on the emotions which are whirling around in your mind. What is the dominant emotion? Is it stress or anxiety? Is it anger, annoyance or frustration? Are you feeling neglected? Are you feeling lonely? What's the core emotion you're feeling?

P: And then the O?

S: Observe. Observe your thought patterns. Which thoughts keep circulating around your mind? Are you having any new thoughts? Are they helping neutralise the negative thoughts or simply adding energy and momentum to them? Are you controlling your thoughts or are they controlling you?

P: And the P?

S: Practice. Practice a fit and healthy mind exercise. Access the oxygen of your positive thoughts, rather than circulating toxic negative ones. Draw on those strong and resilient mental muscles that can help manage these negative emotions. Tap into your mind's flexibility to consider alternative options and outcomes. Exercise lean mental muscles, rather than languishing in flabby negative emotions.

P: And how would you do that?

S: One way is by using the 'Ill at Es to Healthy Ps' technique we looked at earlier. And there are a couple of other techniques we can go through later.

P: So just summarising, STOP is:
>   Stop (everything)
>   Time-out
>   Observe (your thought patterns)
>   Practice (a fit and healthy mind exercise)

Do you have any examples of its application?

STOP example

S: I could quote a couple of examples per day! But let me share something that happened recently. I was worrying about completing lots of work projects which had all landed at the same time, wanting to do them all to a high standard and within the tight deadlines. I was concerned I'd taken too much on and kept waking up at 5.00 in the morning with my mind already whirring about how I was going to cope (or wasn't!). I was convincing myself that at least by waking at this early hour my mind was beginning to work on the problem and I'd come up with better ways of managing everything. The reality was that I was just getting more tired and stressed and less able to think things through clearly.

P: So how did you apply STOP Thinking?

S: Step one was literally telling myself to Stop. Stop the same useless thought patterns. Stop worrying about the situation. Stop stressing.

   The next was Time-out to reflect on my feelings and emotions. I felt anxious as to whether I'd be able to do a good quality job. I felt fear that I might not be able to deliver all the projects on time. And I felt regret that I'd taken too much on and wasn't enjoying the work.

P: What about the next step, Observe?

S: I took a mental step back to observe the thoughts that were flying around in my mind. I tried to slow down my thoughts and to visualise them as clouds rising and falling. This is a useful way to separate yourself from your thoughts and see them in a more detached and objective way. It also means you can observe which thoughts are constantly re-circulating like cases on an airport luggage belt. This helped isolate what was causing the negative emotions.

P: And the final step of Practice a fit and healthy mind exercise?

S: I used a couple of techniques. First was 'Ill at Es to Healthy Ps'. This helped me realise I was getting caught up in my own Ego-fuelled Expectations and helped me get a better sense of Perspective. I also used 'Un-CLOG the Mind' which we can look at later.

This helped me to realise I was creating a sense of catastrophe out of nothing and was also generalising my inability to manage projects to a completely disproportionate level compared with the reality.

P: And did it help?

S: Enormously. I'm not claiming that all my worries instantly evaporated. But it definitely accelerated my ability to stop worrying, to think more clearly and to start to feel more positively about the situation. I have also stored this outcome in my mental muscle memory, so next time a similar situation threatens to occur, I will be better equipped to STOP it before it takes root.

Observing thought patterns

P: The third step of 'Observe your thought patterns' sounds similar to meditation.

S: That's the inspiration behind it. You can term it 'observe your thought patterns', 'gain control of your thoughts', 'mindfulness' or 'meditation'. It's all about viewing your thoughts and thought patterns in a more objective and detached way.

P: So is this about sitting cross-legged in a saffron robe?!

S: Not at all. You can sit cross-legged, open-legged, straight-legged or in any legged (or non-legged) position you want! And in fact you don't need to sit. You can stand or lie. And in terms of what you wear, if purple robes are more your style, you go with that! Wear whatever you want. And if you prefer to do it without any clothes, feel free. Just not when I'm around!

P: Don't worry! I won't subject you to that. Can we dig a bit deeper into this topic of thought patterns?

S: Sure. We tend to consider our thoughts and our mind as one and the same. We consider that our thoughts are our mind naturally working things out in the way that's right for us. But this misses a big opportunity. Which is that we can choose what we think. And since we are what we think, we can choose the 'we who we want to be'.

Choose the 'we who we want to be'

P: Are you suggesting changing our personality?

S: Not in terms of being someone we're not. But as we discussed at the start, there are many versions of you that you can be. Happy you. Sad you. Relaxed you. Worried you. Calm you. Angry you. Jealous you. Contented you. This is about being more of the you that you want to be and less of the you that you don't. It's about recognising that you don't need to think in a negative way. The thoughts that spring into your mind don't need to be the thoughts that you have. Just because thoughts naturally spring up doesn't make them naturally right. You have a choice.

It's the same as choosing the physical version of you that you want to be. Fit you. Out of breath you. Slim you. Overweight you. Sprinting you. Lumbering you. For both the body and mind you have a choice.

P: Meaning?

S: You choose whether you control your thoughts or they control you. You choose whether you're in control of your emotions or hostage to them. Once you accept that your mind and your thoughts are two separate things, you can begin to shape the thoughts which your mind has.

P: So going back to what we were discussing earlier, how do you observe your thought patterns?

Meditation

S: We won't go into too much detail about different meditation and mindfulness approaches as there's lots of material in books and on the internet. But most follow a number of similar core steps. Firstly you find a quiet space. Then close your eyes and relax your body and mind. Focus your mind on something simple and regular like your breath. Keep doing this for 5-10 minutes. If during this time your mind begins to wander, then bring it back to your breath.

P: What's the point of this?

S: It induces a state of calm to your mind. It starts to rid it of noisy thoughts and feelings. You can then mentally step back and observe the thoughts which are entering your mind. Watch them come in. View them like clouds rising from the sea, going up into the sky and then falling back into the sea. Avoid giving them energy. Don't let them develop, and if they do, don't hold onto them. Just let them emerge, rise and fall.

P: And what does this do?

S: Your mind becomes calmer. You see more clearly which thoughts are dominating your mind. You view the ones which keep reappearing. You see whether they are positive or negative. You see whether they are springing from a fit or unfit mind. Once you have observed your thought patterns in this way, you can easily progress to step four and practice a fit and healthy mind exercise to deal with them.

P: This all sounds very powerful, but I'm not sure how easy it would be to actually do.

S: I agree. It does take practice, but those who meditate or practice mindfulness on a daily basis find they soon begin to see their dominant thought patterns and have greater control over them. And the more experienced they become, the more they can do it wherever and whenever they wish.

P: So do you have to go through a deep meditation to use 'STOP'?

S: Not at all. If you find the practice of meditation helpful, it will make it easier to observe your thought patterns. But you can use 'STOP Thinking' as a standalone quick exercise and still gain huge benefit from it.

P: OK, maybe I'll start to 'STOP'!

Give it a go

The next time you're feeling some kind of heavy negative emotion which is weighing you down and your mind is in 'stuck' mode, try 'STOP Thinking'.

- Stop whatever you're doing. That can be hard in this 24/7 multitasking world, but just do it. Completely stop.
- Time out. Treat yourself to just 5 minutes. That's all it needs.
- Observe your thought patterns. Take the perspective of someone outside your mind looking in and observe which thoughts keep recurring. If you find it helpful, do the exercise with someone else and share with them the thoughts circulating in your mind. It's often easier for someone else to make sense of our confused thought patterns.
- Practice an appropriate fit and healthy mind exercise to help neutralise these unhelpful thoughts:
  - If you see that your negativity is being driven by Ego-fuelled Expectations, practice 'Ill at Es to Healthy Ps'.
  - If your mind is full of negativity, try 'Un-CLOG your Mind'.
  - If you're struggling to see the positives of a situation, practice 'Gratitude v Gaptitude'.

Tips

- Don't try to short circuit the exercise by trying to do 'OP' without 'ST'. You have to commit to Stop and Time-out, even if it's just for a few minutes.
- Capture the positive feeling this exercise gives you. This will encourage you to practice it on a regular basis.

7.5. Un-CLOG your Mind

S: Another useful exercise is to un-CLOG the arteries of your mind. I've based this on some of the cognitive distortions David Burns identified in 'The Feeling Good Handbook'.

As we said when discussing the components of a fit and healthy mind, it helps to have a mind composition which has a high proportion of lean mental muscle and minimal mental fat. It's fat thinking which clogs up our mind's ability to pump positive-filled thoughts, feelings and emotions around to the different mental muscles.

P: So how do you un-CLOG your mind?

S: First we need to recognise the factors which CLOG the mind and cause these blockages. Let's go through them one by one.

Catastrophising

C stands for 'Catastrophising'. This is when our mind automatically starts thinking the worst possible outcomes and scenarios. You might have been turned down for a promotion at work. You then get into a spiral of negative thoughts. The directors obviously don't think I'm very good. If they don't think I'm good enough for this job, maybe they don't think I'm good enough for any other job in the company. That means the only job they think I can do is this one. And I know that the young graduate working for me at the moment will be able to do it better than me in a year's time. Where does that leave me? On the scrap heap. How am I going to keep paying the mortgage? There's nothing else for it, my partner will have to work full-time. And we're going to have to start cutting back. There will be no overseas holiday for us this year. And we can say goodbye to that new car we were thinking of buying. And so it goes on...

P: I must admit that's an easy pattern to slip into. And once you start down that negative catastrophic thought spiral it's hard to get back into a positive frame of mind. What about the next one?

Labelling

S: L stands for 'Labelling'. This is using shorthand stereotypes to classify people and situations in a negative and derogatory way. It's a negative mental caricaturing. In the work situation we were just discussing, we might label the person who got the job we wanted as a 'career creep'. The boss may be labelled as a 'naïve judge' and the young up and coming graduate as a 'jumped-up jerk'. We may refer to the interview process as 'more fixed than a Zimbabwean election' and we may now label the new job as 'sounding grander than it actually is'.

P: Do you think labelling is something we really do that regularly?

S: Here's a quick test. Write down the names of 5 people from work and put next to each a short description based on what first comes into your mind. What type of terms have you used? How many of them have negative labels? You can do the same exercise when you walk out of a restaurant, meeting or event. Recall 5 people you noticed and the snapshot label you applied to them.

P: OK you're right. It is something I do a lot and totally subconsciously. But what's the big problem with labelling people and things this way? It can be fun.

S: There's nothing wrong with using a shorthand term to describe someone, as long as it's not negative. But where it's negative labelling, that's the result of unhealthy thinking and is a subconscious attempt to protect our fragile sense of self. By using negative labelling we are often seeking to elevate ourselves. It's trying to buffer ourselves from the reality with fat thoughts, rather than squaring up with strong mental muscles. Also, it means we're storing negativity in our minds, which leads to a mind composition with excess mental fat.

P: What's the third CLOG factor?

Oughtism

S: O stands for 'Oughtism'. This is the unhealthy mental habit of using the term 'Ought'. I *ought* to invite her. I *ought* to send her a present. We *ought* to visit them. You *ought* to study harder. They *ought* to have served us quicker.

'Ought' has a close friend, which is 'Should'. We *should* do more exercise. I *should* learn a new language. You *should* spend more time working in the garden. I *shouldn't* have said that to him. She *shouldn't* have left me on my own.

P: These are pretty regular everyday terms. So I *ought* to ask why we *shouldn't* use them!

S: Because they're emanating from a mind encumbered by a sense of box-ticking, duty, obligation and regret. This is not a fit and healthy mind. They're not driven by a desire to enjoy life, but rather to fulfil a series of duties to oneself and others. And when they're used in the past tense, '*oughtn't* have' and '*shouldn't* have', they are loaded with negative emotions of blame and regret.

They come from being 'Ill at Es'. An Ego-driven Expectation of how the world *ought* to be or *oughtn't* to be. Superimposing our mind's view on how the world *should* be.

Activities such as inviting people, visiting people, sending presents and studying needn't be viewed as duties. They're opportunities to connect and be connected, to experience the positive feelings of giving and to deepen knowledge and understanding.

P: I guess I wouldn't want to be on the receiving end of an '*ought*' or '*should*'. To think that someone is only doing something for me out of a sense of obligation or duty, rather than because they positively and genuinely want to. That they're feeling they *ought* to invite me for dinner, or *ought* to buy me a birthday card.

S: That's an interesting way of viewing it. By exercising a fit and healthy mind you can change all the '*oughts*' and '*shoulds*' to positive intentions which will mean you perform exactly the same activity, but in a more enjoyable and enriching way. Actually in many cases you will perform it to an even greater level because of your positive orientation.

P: What about the final CLOG factor?

Generalising the negative

S: G is for 'Generalising the negative'. This is where we tend to over-generalise and amplify the negatives of a situation and gloss over the positives. The watch-out words which indicate generalising are '*always*' and '*never*'.

Our teenage son or daughter may be playing music at a loud volume one evening. Our reaction is: 'turn that music down, you're *always* playing it at a deafening volume'. Or our partner may have burnt the potatoes. Our reaction is: 'can't you cook anything? You're *always* burning the dinner'. Or our child leaves their bag in the hallway. Our reaction is: 'you *never* put anything away'. Or there may be no milk left in the fridge. Our reaction is: 'you *never* think about anyone else'.

Our minds become distorted in their sense of perspective. Isolated negative events tend to become magnified so we lose our sense of mental balance.

Mind CLOG example

P: This is interesting. I guess I was experiencing mind CLOG the other week. I was travelling from Europe to Asia and my luggage failed to make the connecting flight.

S: What was happening in terms of CLOG thinking?

P: First was definitely Catastrophising. What am I going to do? All my clothes and papers will have gone missing. I'll never remember everything that was in the suitcase for the insurance claim. I'll need to spend weeks finding the old receipts. I'll definitely lose out, that's what always happens with insurance claims. How am I going to manage for tomorrow's meeting? They'll think I'm really unprofessional. There's no way we'll get the contract if I turn up totally unshaven with the same jeans I've been wearing for the last 48 hours. And so it went on.

S: What about Labelling?

P: I was doing plenty of that. It was those 'disorganised Indonesians' who didn't co-ordinate the baggage. It was the French baggage workers who were 'drinking coffee and smoking Gitanes' rather than making sure my luggage was onboard. I was 'stupid' expecting my luggage to make three tight connecting flights.

S: Any Oughtism?

P: Of course. The airlines *ought* to make sure all the baggage is on the flight before it takes off. The airports *should* get better systems to track luggage. The baggage handlers *ought* to take greater care with people's property. I really *ought* to have packed some essentials in my carryon luggage. I *should* have taken a note of what I packed to make an insurance claim.

S: What about Generalising?

P: I do recall thinking my baggage *always* gets lost, baggage handlers *never* take enough care, I *always* have problems when I'm travelling and airlines *never* keep you informed of what's happening.

S: So how were you feeling with all this CLOG thinking?

P: Pretty cross and frustrated. Also worried and disappointed. A whole mixture of emotions which kept swirling around in my mind. Overall, fairly stressed out about the whole situation.

S: It's only when we step back that we realise CLOG thinking is something we do quite frequently. Maybe not always as dramatically as when your baggage went missing and maybe not always involving all four factors. But just count the number of times each day you use the terms 'ought', 'should', 'always' and 'never'. That will give you some indication of the extent of your CLOG thinking.

P: So back to my earlier question, what can you do to un-CLOG your mind?

Un-CLOG your mind - Catastrophising

S: Here are a few mini exercises that can help. You can view them as mental press-ups to overcome the mental hang-ups.

Let's start with Catastrophising. There's a short mental routine you can go through when you feel your mind spiralling into Catastrophising mode. It involves going through the following 7 de-Catastrophisation steps:

1. What am I Catastrophising may happen?
2. What is the worst that could happen?
3. How likely is this to happen?
4. What are the consequences of this?
5. Are there any positives of this scenario?
6. What is most likely to happen?
7. How serious really is this?

Capture this new reality and hold it in your mind. It's like holding a physical exercise position or muscle position.

P: Let's go through the 7 de-Catastrophisation steps with my lost luggage:

1. I was Catastrophising about losing my clothes, losing the contract and losing my reputation.
2. I guess the worst that could happen is the suitcase would be lost forever.
3. The likelihood of this is probably less than 5%.

4. The consequences are that I would have to buy new clothes, toiletries…and a new suitcase! And then claim them back on the insurance.
5. The positives of this are that I could update my clothes, many of which are getting a bit worn anyway. And I'd get a new suitcase to replace the rather battered one I've dragged around the world.
6. The most likely scenario is my luggage will be delivered later that day.
7. That wouldn't be too serious as I'm not due to have the meeting until the next day. So I could pop out to the local shops to buy some clothes for the next day just in case.

S: So out of interest what did happen?

P: The suitcase was delivered to my hotel room 6 hours later! All that worry proved totally unnecessary and unproductive!

S: That's the thing with Catastrophising. It really is a lot of wasted mental effort, caused by fat thinking and stimulating more fat thinking.

Un-CLOG your mind - Labelling

Let's look at a technique to help deal with Labelling. As soon as you realise you're labelling people or situations, quickly exercise your mind to find three positive descriptors to counteract the negative ones. Capture those and hold them in your mind.

P: I used the term 'disorganised Indonesians'. I guess I could counteract this with more positive descriptors such as 'flexible', 'friendly' and 'resourceful'.

S: Does this change your view of them?

P: I guess it does. It creates a more positive feeling in my mind when I think of them in this less jaundiced way. Strangely, I also feel more positive towards myself, eliminating this negativity from my mind.

Un-CLOG your mind - Oughtism

S: Let's move onto Oughtism. A useful exercise is to replace the Oughtism phrase with a fit and healthy mind expression. So instead of 'I *ought* to invite her', rephrase it as 'she would really enjoy meeting some new people and I would gain a sense of satisfaction from seeing her socialise more'. Or instead of 'I *should* learn a new language', reframe it as 'it would be interesting to learn a new language so I can get a deeper understanding of a different country and culture'.

P: I said 'airlines *ought* to make sure all the baggage is on the flight before it takes off'. How might I reframe that?

S: What is it that's driving you to use the term '*ought*'? It's back to being 'Ill at Es' again. Our Ego-fuelled Expectation as to how the world *ought* to be.
  But if we move to Healthy Ps, we see things in a different light. Many People are doing everything they can to ensure the luggage gets onto all the flights. With a sense of Perspective, we can see it's relatively rare that luggage actually goes missing and considering the complexity of airline operations and scheduling, together with all the security and weather issues they also have to contend with, it's amazing that it doesn't go missing more frequently. And looking at the Positive, we can be grateful that it was only our

luggage that went missing and not us!

Un-CLOG your mind – Generalising the negative

P: So finally, is there an exercise to help overcome Generalising the negative?

S: Yes, it's similar to the one for Labelling. Just think of three recent incidences where the generalisation does not apply. Where your teenager has played music at a low volume or worn earphones. Where your partner has cooked meals without burning them. Where your child has put things away. Where there has been milk in the fridge. Then hold this mental position.

P: With the example of my luggage and my negative generalisation that it *always* gets lost, if I'm honest, it doesn't. In fact it has never got lost before! It has got delayed twice in the last year, but then that isn't too bad when I consider I've taken more than 30 flights.

S: So you can see that un-CLOG your mind is quite an easy and effective exercise to practice.

P: I'd like to say 'I *ought* to give it a go'!

Give it a go

- Un-CLOG your mind is a great technique to use either to manage a specific CLOG, or as a general mind health and fitness check, as explained here:
- Choose a day when you want to check your mind CLOG.
- Live the day in your normal way, but make a written note every time you notice CLOGs in your mind.
- At the end of the day assess the extent of your mind CLOG.
- How often did you Catastrophise? What was it about? How warranted was it?
- To what extent did you use Labelling? What negative images did you allow to infiltrate your mind?
- How much of what you thought or said was Oughtism based? What was driving that? Was it pressure of time? Was it a desire to superimpose your Ego and your Expectations?
- Did you tend to Generalise the negative? Did you find yourself ascribing terms such as 'always' and 'never' when something wasn't in line with your Expectations?
- Now go through each of the CLOGs and start to un-CLOG your mind.
- Look at what you were Catastrophising about. Is it still as much of a disaster as you had conceived earlier? If not, hold that thought so your mind becomes less prone to Catastrophisation in future. If so, use the 7 de-Catastrophisation steps to assess the situation in a more balanced and objective way.
- Reflect on the negative Labels you created. For each of these, find three positive descriptors.

- Consider each of the Oughtisms. Rephrase them in a way that's reflective of a mind that believes in life enjoyment, for yourself and everyone else.
- Think about each occasion you Generalised the negative. For each, think of three occasions which show this negative generalisation to be misplaced.
- How does that feel? Does your mind feel a lot freer, a lot less weighty, a lot more at one with yourself and the world? Capture the feeling. Capture the thought patterns which have got you there. Store those in your memory to secure that feeling.

Tips

- You can use the individual elements of Un-CLOG your Mind as soon as you notice a particular type of CLOG arise. The most frequent and most pervasive ones are Catastrophising and Oughtism.
- Become aware of mind CLOGs in others. Use the techniques in a kind and supportive way to help them un-CLOG their mind.

7.6. Change It or Change I

S: We've discussed how enjoyment is not about the external, but our internal response to the external. I've put together a little exercise to remind myself of this. It's called 'Change It or Change I'. It's based on a fundamental principle of Buddhism and again exercises all 5 components of a fit and healthy mind.

When something isn't what I'd like it to be, I ask myself the question: 'Change It or Change I?' If it's easy and positively healthy to Change It, the external situation, then that's what I'll do. But if it's easier and actually healthier to Change I, I'll do that.

P: Do you want to give me an example?

'Change It or Change I' example

S: It might be a simple everyday situation like my son not doing his homework. Here I will look to Change It. In a fit and healthy mind way of course, rather than getting angry and ranting on at him. But I'll point out to him the benefits of doing his school work, or help him with it or promise we'll do something together as soon as he gets it finished.

But another everyday situation may be his leaving stuff all over his bedroom floor. Here I may decide to Change I. To change the way I view it. To no longer be irritated by it. But to view it that he has a lot of other things on his mind (including the homework I'm now encouraging him to complete!) and that this will not make much material difference to his or my life, either now or in the future.

P: This may have been a useful technique during that disastrous holiday in France. I was totally fixated on Change It. Change the resort, change the weather, change the rep, change the food and change the French! If I'd taken the route of Change I and changed the way I was viewing and responding to these external stimuli, I would have had a much more enjoyable holiday.

S: Another example would be if my son was driving dangerously fast. This would definitely be a case of Change It. But if I'm worrying about his driving after midnight, based on nothing other than my own Catastrophising mind, I'll look to Change I.

P: Does this link again with the 'Ill at Es to Healthy Ps' technique?

Link to 'Ill at Es to Healthy Ps'

S: Yes, because 'Ill at Es' is often what causes us to try to Change It, when it would be more appropriate to Change I. We try to superimpose our Ego-driven Expectations on how the world should be. We then experience negative Emotions when things don't comply with our paradigm. Change I comes from a 'Healthy Ps' mindset. One that considers other People's views as well as our own; one that has a balanced Perspective and the Positivity to appreciate that enjoyment most often comes from changing our response, rather than always trying to change the external.

P: I can also see it would be a useful exercise when having a disagreement with someone. The temptation is always to Change It, but often it may be better to Change I, to actually change the way I am viewing the situation.

S: It can also help to make the expression more

personalised. So phrase it as: 'Change He or Change Me?' or 'Change She or Change Me?' This helps to reinforce that too often we're trying to change another person, rather than accepting them and seeking to change that which is in our greater remit of control, which is ourselves and our response.

P: But is this not a sign of weakness, bending to other people's views all the time rather than looking to enforce our own?

S: It's not all the time. A fit and healthy mind will be able to discern those times when Change It is the best approach and when it's healthier to Change I. Having the ability to Change I is actually a sign of mental strength and power. It's also healthier and importantly leads to a more enjoyable life. The best proof is to try it out for yourself.

P: That will mean Change I, literally! But I think I might give it a go...

Give it a go

'Change It or Change I' can be used countless times in the day.

- Choose the next moment you're experiencing any kind of negative thoughts or feelings.
- Capture what that thought or feeling is.
- Now think about changing what you identify as the external stimulus – it may be a person or thing.
- How easily can the external stimulus be changed? How right is it that the external stimulus changes? How fit and healthy is your mind in wanting it to change?
- Now think about yourself. How easily could the way you are perceiving the external stimulus be changed? Would that be easier than the stimulus changing? Would it be more appropriate than the stimulus changing? To what extent are you exercising a fit and healthy mind?

Tips

- On occasions, this technique will lead you to the fit and healthy mind conclusion that it's appropriate that the external stimulus changes. It's helpful to then make that change in a fit and healthy mind way.
- In the majority of occasions, the most appropriate change will be to our minds. And the benefit will be a genuinely greater level of enjoyment and a fitter and healthier mind going forward.

7.7. Challearnge Yourself

S: There is a risk with this approach to enjoying life that you allow life to become quite mundane. You could say to yourself that since enjoyment comes from the internal reaction to the external, there's no need to do anything particularly stimulating from an external point of view. But this is not what enjoying life by exercising a fit and healthy mind is about.

P: Go on.

S: We need to set a positive intent each day to enjoy life by exercising a fit and healthy mind. So our first priority is to enjoy the day and to enjoy each moment of the day. This means actively looking for ways in which to make it fully enriching and enjoyable. Part of this is stepping out of our natural comfort zone and trying new things. Going to new places, meeting new people, trying new activities, exploring different career options etc.

P: Is this not looking for enjoyment from external stimuli?

Positive stimulus

S: This is quite a finely balanced point. We need to recognise that going to new places will not of itself provide us with any enjoyment. In fact, we may feel disappointed. Likewise, meeting new people will not of itself provide us with enjoyment. We may instead feel anxious or insecure. New things can, however, provide a positive stimulus which, depending on our internal reaction, can provide enhanced enjoyment.

P: Is this like trying new physical exercises? You need

to stimulate the body with different physical exercises otherwise your health and fitness simply plateaus.

S: Yes, it's about getting out there and touching life. Not because the external stimuli will of themselves provide enjoyment. But because they provide a richer set of experiences which, with a fit and healthy mind, we can choose to respond to in a way which invigorates and enriches our life enjoyment. I've termed this: 'Challearnge yourself'.

P: Is that a mispronunciation?

S: Yes, a deliberate one. What often holds us back from taking on new challenges and experiences is the risk of failure. No one likes failure. It makes us feel inadequate. It acts as a barrier to trying new things in the future.

Challearnge yourself

P: And yet often when we do actually pluck up the courage to try new things we really enjoy them and wonder why we held ourselves back.

S: That's the point. We need to develop a mindset that says that whatever the outcome, taking the challenge was a good decision. That's why it's termed 'Challearnge yourself'. It's a combination of challenge and learn. Take the challenge and learn from it. That way you always win.

P: Expand a bit more.

S: Whenever you're faced with a new challenge or experience, say to yourself that however it turns out, I'm going to learn from this. If it turns out well, you've learnt a new skill or learnt about a new person or place. And most importantly, you've learnt that taking new challenges can be rewarding. This is a key learning to store in your mind, so that the next time you're contemplating whether to take a challenge, you're more positively inclined, because you recall the previous positive outcome.

P: And when they don't go well?

S: You can still enjoy them because you've learnt something from the experience. At its most extreme, you've learnt never to do that activity again! But more likely, especially when exercising a fit and healthy mind, you've learnt that it's actually OK. You can do it, albeit not to a high standard yet. You didn't look stupid. You didn't totally clam up. You weren't totally inadequate. You were enriched by it.

Or you may have learnt that you can't run a marathon, but that you could comfortably run 2km. And with a little bit of training, you could run 5km, progressing to 10km. Or you may have learnt you can't win the tennis tournament, but that you can get into the quarter-finals. Or that actually just playing social tennis is really enjoyable, without the need to enter any tournaments. Or that you can't get the top job, but that you can achieve a well-paid middle management position. Or that actually you would prefer to stay with your current role.

P: This sounds as if it's grounded again in 'Ill at Es to Healthy Ps'. It's our fragile Ego and high self-Expectation that lead us to avoid new challenges in case we fail. The spiral of negative Emotions around failure convinces us not to try anything outside of our comfort zone.

S: Yes. Whereas 'Healthy Ps' helps us to realise that

all People try things and fail. With a sense of Perspective, it really doesn't matter. And if we apply Positive thinking, we can appreciate what we've learnt from the experience and be enriched by it.

P: But is that not potentially selfish? Pursuing our personal challenges with no regard for those who may be impacted?

S: It comes back to intention. What is our motivation? If it is the pursuit of something for purely selfish ends, yes this is questionable. But if we are exercising a fit and healthy mind, this is unlikely to be our intent. We won't be driven purely by Ego, but will take full account of other People as well.

No such thing as failure

P: What you seem to be saying from all this is that there's no such thing as failure.

S: That's the key point. What is failure? Performing below someone's Ego-driven Expectation, leading to negative Emotions. If we reframe everything into a Challearnge, and approach it with a fit and healthy mind, there is no failure. There's simply an opportunity to try something new or different from which we can gain both enjoyment and learning.

P: So the only failure is failing to Challearnge yourself!

Give it a go

Challearnge yourself is a great technique to use whenever you feel yourself saying 'no' to a new opportunity.

- Look out for the next time there's an opportunity to do something new or a bit different and you find your natural reaction is 'no'. We're not talking here about taking excessive physical or financial risks, just things that others do and we shy away from.
- Think about why it is that you're seeking reasons not to do it. Fear of failure? Fear of making a fool of yourself? Fear of embarrassment? Fear of not being able to cope, physically or mentally? Fear of becoming a burden to others? Fear of letting yourself and others down?
- Then say 'yes'. Say 'yes' to yourself. Say 'yes' to the person offering. Say 'yes' to the opportunity.
- Having committed yourself by saying 'yes', your mind may later become filled with all the negatives. You may think of all the things that could go wrong and you'll be tempted to say 'no', to politely decline, to find an excuse.
- This is a good time to use the 'STOP Thinking' exercise. Stop whatever you're doing. Take time-out for a few minutes to capture what you're feeling. Observe the negative thoughts circulating around your mind. Practice this 'Challearnge yourself' exercise.
- Say to yourself: 'I'm going to give this a try'. Put aside your Expectation-driven Ego and your Ego-driven Expectation. Tell yourself that it's your life and you can have a go at doing anything you want. Think about the worst eventuality that could arise from you taking on the challenge. Now go and do it.

- How was it? Was it a total disaster? Most probably not. Was it actually quite enjoyable? Probably so. Hold that memory for next time, so you're more open to accepting the next challenge that comes your way.
- And whatever the experience, capture the learning. It may simply be to say 'yes' to opportunities more often. It may be to develop a particular skill or competency to make it easier next time.
- Celebrate the fact that you've Challearnged yourself and enjoyed life a little bit more as a result.

Tips

- Try it first with an easy challenge and then build up to something more extreme.
- Ensure you capture the learning each time. This will make future challenges seem more like normal everyday events.
- Remember of course that it's not the external challenge which is providing the enjoyment. It is still the internal response of our minds to a different external stimulus, which is making life more fulfilling, enriching and enjoyable.

7.8. Mentathalon

S: Sometimes we deal with difficult people or situations by avoiding or running away from them. Which means we're not dealing with them. It's like a physically unfit person never feeling out of breath or physically exerted, because they avoid any form of strenuous activity. Or someone who goes to the gym, but spends the whole time sitting on an exercise machine, whilst reading a magazine or watching the TV.

P: And what's the problem with avoiding difficult people and situations?

S: It means we're getting through life, rather than fully enjoying it. We're just coping with life or managing it, rather than really enjoying it. At some point we run the risk of having a nasty shock because we haven't built up the required mental strength and stamina. What I've found useful in these situations is an exercise which I've termed 'Mentathalon'.

P: So what exactly is that?

Become like an athlete

S: In the same way as an athlete would enter a physically gruelling series of events, we can do the same with our minds. We put ourselves into the heart of an emotionally charged environment and see how well we can tough it out. We accept it will test our mental positivity to the extreme. We recognise it will push our mental muscles to their limits and maybe beyond. We acknowledge it may stretch our mental flexibility to near breaking point. But, viewing it as an athlete would an event, mentally preparing for it.

115

Welcoming it as a Challearnge. Experiencing it and learning from the experience and being stronger as a result.

P: Could you give me an example?

S: Think of someone who you find difficult to be with.

P: OK, now what?

S: How would you normally manage being with that person?

P: Most of the time I'd avoid being with him or her! But when I've got no choice, I'd grin and bear it. I'd bite my lip and just try to endure it, counting the hours until I could get away.

S: So not very enjoyable?!

P: No! But it's more a matter of keeping the peace and making sure the whole situation doesn't explode. So how would you suggest approaching it with this Mentathalon mindset?

Entering a Mentathalon

S: Say to yourself: 'I'm going to enjoy this time by exercising the fit and healthy mind which I've developed. In fact, I'm going to use it to develop an even fitter and healthier mind, which will help me enjoy this time and be better prepared for other challenging times in the future. It may be tough, but it will give me that sense of achievement that athletes enjoy having accomplished a physically demanding series of events'.

P: How would that work through from a practical point

of view?

S: So you're in the situation. Every time you start to feel negative thoughts coming into your mind, pump positive-filled thoughts, feelings and emotions around to the different mental muscles. Visualise yourself in a mental gym, where you're working your mental muscles to extremes, building their strength and resilience. See yourself in a mental yoga class, developing more mental flexibility and stretch, whilst retaining your mental poise, balance and core stability. Feel energised by the mental fat you're burning off and mental muscle you're building up. After the event, clock your recovery time. Note how long it is before you feel composed and mentally at rest again.

P: And you think that will help?

S: I know from my personal experience it definitely does. It makes the challenging situation more enjoyable and builds you up mentally to more easily handle similar challenges in the future.

P: I now want to find a challenging person! Where are they when you're looking for them?!

S: I'm not far away!

Give it a go

Become a Mentathlete.

- Identify a Mentathalon event. A person or situation that you find emotionally demanding and exhausting, and would normally seek to avoid.
- Prepare yourself beforehand. Fill your mind with positive thoughts. Work up your mental strength and resilience. Limber up a flexible and balanced mind.
- Enter the Mentathalon.
- Try to convert every negative thought or feeling into a positive. Feel your mental muscles becoming stronger and more resilient. Feel your mind increasing in its flexibility and adaptability, whilst retaining its poise and balance.
- At the end, take a deep breath and congratulate yourself.
- Hold that positive, strengthened feeling.
- Enjoy the greater fitness of mind you have now developed.

Tips

- Don't be disheartened if you don't manage to stay positive and mentally strong throughout. You will have built a stronger base for the future.
- Try to see every emotionally charged situation, which you'd previously avoided or dreaded, as a Mentathalon event. It will make it more bearable, even enjoyable, and you will significantly develop the health and fitness of your mind.

8. ENJOYING LIFE IN PRACTICE

S: So that's what 'Enjoy Life by Exercising a Fit and Healthy Mind' is all about. It has at its core a completely different way of viewing life. It recognises that enjoyment, true enjoyment, does not come from the external, but from our internal response to the external.

On the one hand that is debilitating. It means we can't find enjoyment from just getting more stuff. But as we've discussed, that's an illusory form of enjoyment anyway. In fact the approach is completely liberating. No longer are we dependent on external circumstances for our life enjoyment. Enjoyment is fundamentally within our control. All day, every day.

P: Just to confirm, you're saying what goes on around us has no impact on our enjoyment of life?

Positive external stimulus

S: As we said earlier, positive external stimulus can make it easier to enjoy life than negative external stimulus. So sunny weather may be a better stimulus to having an enjoyable day than wind and rain, but it's no guarantee. Many unenjoyable experiences happen in the most beautiful of weather and many of the most enjoyable in the worst of weather. If we're looking to the weather as our source of enjoyment, we are reliant upon the external rather than the fitness of our own minds. Likewise, a car which works is a better stimulus to having an enjoyable life than a car which breaks down. But again it's no guarantee.

P: So you're suggesting that positive external stimulus is a good thing.

S: Yes, as long as we keep in mind two important points. The first is to recognise that external stimulus is not the cause of enjoyment or unenjoyment. It is simply something happening around us, to which we can then choose how we're going to respond. Remember the 90/10 principle. Only 10% of our enjoyment is attributable to the external; 90% is down to the internal response of our mind. Secondly, we need to be careful that we don't become reliant on it. If we always surround ourselves with positive stimulus, we won't develop our mental fitness. The moment we are presented with negative external stimulus we won't have the capacity to manage it and so will find ourselves unable to enjoy life and unable to easily identify why and how to cope.

P: But how easy is it to enjoy life in this way?

Needs exercise

S: It needs the exercising of a fit and healthy mind. A mind that is oxygenated with positive thoughts rather than toxic negative ones. A mind that has developed strong and resilient mental muscles that can resist negative emotions like stress, anger and jealousy. A flexible mind that can more easily respond to different challenges in a fluid and adaptable, but balanced way. And finally, a mind that is lean and lucid rather than flabby and overburdened with the baggage of previous unhealthy thoughts.

P: But that doesn't come easily.

S: Agreed. But developing a fit and healthy mind is in itself enjoyable. It's enjoyable to flood your mind with positive thoughts. Developing stronger and more resilient mental muscles gives you a great sense of achievement, whilst building the basis for greater enjoyment in the future. Flexible thinking will be rewarded by new options and experiences and will be appreciated by those around you. And finally, a lean mind will be able to face life's challenges and opportunities with a renewed sense of vigour and potency.

P: So you're saying it's not that hard to put into practice?

S: At one level, no. There's nothing intrinsically complex or arduous about the exercises. They're quick and easy. They can be used at anytime, wherever you are. It's not an all or nothing approach. You can use them as little or as much as you like. And they work. Instantly.

P: So what's the more challenging aspect?

Challenging aspect

S: That our minds have been hardwired during our lifetimes to see the world in a particular way. We consider it the right and only way, because that's the way we think. But just because we think a particular way doesn't make it naturally right. Especially if it's actually counterproductive to enjoying life. So the more challenging (or Challearnging as we now say!) aspect is having the self-honesty and self-willingness to open our minds to a new way of thinking. To a new natural. And to have the inner strength to keep getting back on track when we slip back into old thinking.

P: Is there any advice on how to do this?

S: Having the right overall intent is key. Remember, and keep reminding yourself, that the overall goal is to have a fully enjoyable life. It's as clear, simple and fundamental as that. Nothing more, nothing less. So keep checking with yourself: 'Am I enjoying life?', 'Am I enjoying it as much as I could?', 'Am I living in the now and is it an enjoyable now?' Then keep reminding yourself that the only route to achieving this goal is by exercising a fit and healthy mind.

P: Is there a risk this becomes overbearing? That you become so focused on trying to enjoy life that you don't? Or on trying to develop a fit and healthy mind that you actually make it unfit and unhealthy?

Pace yourself

S: You're right. Again the parallels from developing physical fitness are helpful. If we become obsessive in developing a fit and healthy body, this can become counterproductive. We become physically exhausted, our muscles ache and become prone to injury, our bodies stiffen up. This puts us out of action and we start to lose our leanness and put on excess fat. In the same way, we need to approach the development of a fit and healthy mind in the right way.

P: What do you mean?

S: To recognise that our mind will never be 100% fit and healthy. That we will always have worries and concerns. That there will be times of irritation and anger. That we'll have feelings of jealousy and disappointment.

P: So what's the point of trying to develop a fit and healthy mind?

S: Because you will experience these negative emotions less intensively and less frequently. In their place you will experience the more positive emotions of happiness and contentedness, of enrichment and fulfilment. And you will experience them more fully and more frequently.

P: Are there any other parallels with developing physical fitness?

S: If you're in an unfit physical condition, you don't immediately look to run a marathon or climb Mount Kilimanjaro. You start by gradually building up the different components of physical fitness. You take encouragement from the progress you've made compared to when you started and how it's giving you a greater overall sense of vigour and potency. If it's getting too intense or you're not enjoying it, you take a day off. If you're starting to ache you knock down the intensity a level or two. It's the same with developing a fit and healthy mind.

P: Is this what you've done?

S: Yes and still do. As I mentioned earlier, I started from a position of being easily irritated by things, worrying about work pressures, thinking enjoyment was in the external. So I started in a fairly unhealthy position. But by setting an overall intent to enjoy life and gradually using the different exercises, I've made huge strides forward.

But some days I became too focused on trying to enjoy myself, which was having a counterproductive effect. So I backed off a bit. Other times I got too concerned with applying the exercises all the time. So I chilled a little and picked them up again when I felt ready. Other times I've become frustrated that I still have worries, still get irritated and still have feelings of jealousy. But I've accepted that these negative emotions will never be totally eradicated and that if I can just maintain the progress I've already achieved in minimising them, that will lead to a significantly more enjoyable life.

Mental health issues

P: What about people who have serious mental health problems?

S: It's better that they firstly consult a medical expert. As with physical health and fitness, if you have a broken leg there's no point trying to repair it by just getting yourself down the gym and doing some exercises. You need to firstly have the fracture correctly assessed, an operation carried out and then be given a series of prescribed exercises. It's the same principle with trying to repair a mentally unhealthy mind.

P: So if it's not for those with serious mental health issues, who is it for?

S: Everyone else! Anyone who experiences worry, stress, anger, upset, jealousy and the whole range of negative emotions which get in the way of enjoying life. And that is everyone. Admittedly, some may experience these emotions less intensely than others or they may consider their lives to be perfectly enjoyable at the moment. But as John F Kennedy said: 'the best time to repair the roof is when the sun is shining'.

P: Any other tips about enjoying life in practice?

Progressing with others

S: Something which provides a huge boost is having a community of people who share this same goal and approach. You can certainly make huge strides on your own, as indeed I have when seeking to find and develop the approach. And the need for support from others does vary by individual. But for most of us, being part of a group of people who share a common intent really is tremendously motivating. It provides reassurance, encouragement and inspiration.

P: Any downsides?

You are the only benchmark

S: The only thing you need to watch out for, as in all aspects of life, is that you don't make unhelpful comparisons. To want the level of life enjoyment someone else appears to have. There is only one benchmark. And that is yourself. The moment you're making comparisons, is the moment you're stopping enjoying the only life you can enjoy, and that's your's. You're letting Ego, Expectation and Emotion(-ve) enter your mind. You're focusing on Gaptitude rather than Gratitude. So cultivate a sense of community, but as a fountain of encouragement and support, rather than comparison and competition.

P: So why would anyone want to wait before giving it a try?

S: More specifically, why would you?!

9. ENJOY LIFE!

S: So that's it. The rest is up to you. It's your life and so your decision as to the extent to which you want to enjoy it. You don't have to. In fact most people go through life without enjoying it to the full. Mainly because they don't know how.

P: And to get started?

S: Just start. The exercises will guide and help. No need to make any great announcement, or financial investment or resolution. Just start giving it a go. Say to yourself, 'I now want to start enjoying my life to the full. I want to live in the now. I want to recapture the life that is uniquely mine and which I recognise is fast disappearing. I want on my deathbed to be able to say that I have enjoyed my life to the full. I want to liberate my dependency on the external. I want to grasp the opportunity to find enjoyment from my internal response to the external. I want to develop a mind that is more capable of doing that. I want to Enjoy Life by Exercising a Fit and Healthy Mind'.

10. INFLUENCES

The thoughts in this book are the result of many different articles, books, presentations, observations, conversations and experiences over many years. So whilst it is virtually impossible to identify all the influences, I would like to highlight the main ones. Through this, I would also like to give my sincere thanks and gratitude to all those people for their inspiration, different perspectives, challenges and general support.

Firstly Di, my wife, for her unyielding support through all the different thinking phases I've been through during our married life. I hope that through this transformation, I've become a slightly more enjoyable person to live with!

Our children, Ben & Vicky. Ben for his comments on the earliest version of my thoughts and Vicky for the book design. Also for inadvertently providing much of the material relating to the handling of challenging teenagers!

Sam Craddock, my nephew, for initially alerting me to

the five components of physical fitness, which then provided the basis for the analogy with a fit and healthy mind.

My critical reviewers, Rob & Hilary Lucas, Pete & Paula Turton, Sue & Paul Mobey and Esther Routledge. Your comments helped knock off some of the rough and incomprehensible edges, made the content more broadly appealing and contributed some great new exercises and examples.

Kelsang Leksang, from Birmingham Samantabhadra Kadampa Buddhist Centre. For sharing, in her inimitably gentle and humorous style, so many great lessons from Buddhist teaching. A real inspiration in every sense of the word.

All the thought leaders whose material I've read and re-read in my quest for a more enjoyable life. I list them here because directly and indirectly they have been a huge source of guidance and inspiration, not simply during the writing of this book, but in shaping my thinking and approach over many years. They are all sources I fully recommend to any reader who wants to explore this whole topic area further:

> Action for Happiness movement, for seeking to create a happier society for everyone
> James Borg, 'Mind Power'
> David Burns, 'The Feeling Good Handbook'
> Stephen Covey, 'The 7 Habits of Highly Effective People'
> Adrian Furnham, University College London, for your weekly thought pieces in the Sunday Times
> Geshe Kelsang Gyatso, 'Transform Your Life'
> Susan Jeffers, 'Feel the Fear and Do It Anyway'
> Francois Lelord, 'Hector and the Search for

Happiness'
John Naish, 'Enough'
Andy Puddicombe, Headspace, for your
meditation thoughts
Matthieu Ricard, 'Happiness – A Guide to
Developing Life's Most Important Skill'
Robin Sharma, 'The Monk Who Sold His
Ferrari'
David Taylor, Naked Leader, for your mind-
stimulating weekly thought pieces
Bronnie Ware, 'The Top Five Regrets of the
Dying'

11. QUICK REFERENCE EXERCISE GUIDE

1. Energise your Intent

Purpose: to set a positive intent for the day

Key elements:
- Express gratitude
- Recognise that this day is a one-off opportunity
- Commit to exercising your mental muscles during the day, to be both emotionally strong and resilient
- Set an intent to be flexible in your thinking and to retain mental balance and poise
- Commit to using the day to build up more lean mental muscle and burn off unhelpful mental fat

2. Gratitude v Gaptitude

Purpose: to boost your positive thinking fitness by focusing on what you already have

Key elements:
- Train your mind to focus on what you have, rather than on what you don't
- For every Gaptitude that you express, think of 5 related reasons for expressing Gratitude

3. Ill at Es to Healthy Ps

Purpose: to unlock the cause of our negativity and redirect us to a more positive path

Key elements:
- Ill at Es – Ego, Expectation, Emotion(-ve)
- Healthy Ps – People, Perspective, Positive thinking
- Recognise the role of Ego-driven Expectation in creating the negative Emotion
- Consider other People and a broader Perspective to develop more Positive thinking

4. STOP Thinking

Purpose: to get our mind out of 'stuck' mode

Key elements:
- Stop whatever you're doing
- Time-out to reflect on the emotions whirling around in your mind
- Observe the thought patterns which keep circulating
- Practice a fit and healthy mind exercise

5. Un-CLOG your Mind

Purpose: to build up lean mental muscle in place of unhealthy fat thinking

Key elements:
Un-CLOG the following fat thinking:
- Catastrophising – imagining the worst possible outcomes. So practice the 7 de-catastrophisation steps.
- Labelling – classifying people in a negative way. So find 3 positive descriptors.
- Oughtism – doing things out of a sense of duty and obligation. So rephrase to reflect an 'enjoy life' ethos.
- Generalising the negative – focusing on and amplifying the negatives of a situation. So identify 3 counterpoints.

6. Change It or Change I

Purpose: to quickly assess whether it's best to change the external stimulus or change our internal response

Key elements:
- Assess how easy and positively healthy it is to change the external stimulus
- Assess how easy and positively healthy it is to change our internal response
- In most cases, exercising a fit and healthy mind will lead to the decision to Change *I* rather than Change *It*

7. Challearnge Yourself

Purpose: to help step out of our comfort zone and try new things

Key elements:
- When your instinct may be to say 'no', say 'yes'
- Enjoy the experience, whatever the outcome
- Reflect on and capture the learning

8. Mentathalon

Purpose: to develop a much fitter and healthier mind by entering an emotionally challenging situation

Key elements:
- Mentally prepare yourself beforehand
- Turn each negative thought or feeling into a positive
- Feel your mental muscles grow stronger and more resilient
- Experience your mind becoming more flexible
- Enjoy burning off mental fat and building lean mental muscle

ABOUT THE AUTHOR

Steve Mills has always been intrigued by life. What motivates people to live their lives a certain way? Do some people enjoy their lives more than others? Is this down to external or internal factors?

This lifelong fascination has been interwoven with his professional career as an international marketing speaker, working with major global companies. His academic background includes an MBA from Warwick Business School.

Having spent the past 50 years searching for real enjoyment in life, he is now keen to share his approach with others who may find it helpful.